The Road Less Travelled

MEMOIRS OF THE UBEROI FAMILY

The
Road Less
Travelled
MEMOIRS OF
THE UBEROI FAMILY

Rajeev Uberoi

AMARYLLIS

AMARYLLIS

An imprint of Manjul Publishing House Pvt. Ltd.
• C-16, Sector 3, Noida, Uttar Pradesh 201 301, India
Website: www.manjulindia.com
Registered Office:
• 2nd Floor, Usha Preet Complex, 42 Malviya Nagar, Bhopal 462 003 – India
Distribution Centres
Ahmedabad, Bengaluru, Chennai, Hyderabad,
Kochi, Kolkata, Mumbai, Noida, Pune

The Road Less Travelled by *Rajeev Uberoi*

Copyright © Rajeev Uberoi, 2024

Rajeev Uberoi asserts the moral right to be
identified as the author of this work

This edition first published in India in 2024

ISBN 978-93-5543-636-8

Cover Design: pealidezine@gmail.com

Printed and bound in India by Repro India Limited.

This book is dedicated to the loving memory of my beloved parents – Balkrishan and Satish Bala Uberoi

CONTENTS

A map of India prior to 15th August 1947

PREFACE

History has always fascinated me. I enjoy visiting historical sites and reading about them in order to better understand the political, social, economic, cultural, and human aspects of times gone by. I distinctly remember that when I was studying in the Scindia School, which is located within the majestic Gwalior Fort, whenever there was an opportunity to visit the various historical monuments within the fort premises, I would always be the first one to jump up at the chance. Although all public sections of the fort were out of bounds for us, every once in a while we were allowed a conducted tour of some parts under the vigilant eyes of our teachers. Those visits to monuments like the Man Mandir, the Teliki Zat, and the Sasbahu Temple always saw my imagination fly wild and free as I wondered about what all must have happened within the walls of these buildings and how people who lived in those times must have laboured to build such magnificent structures.

Exploring history through a wide range of sources like monuments, documents, paintings, artefacts, and coins that have survived the tests of time not only provides us with a deeper insight into the nature of social, political, economic, cultural, and spiritual life in the yesteryears, but it also gives us an opportunity to look at events from history with a newer perspective. Furthermore, it allows us to develop our own assessments and views about what happened in the past.

It is this passion to know more and more about the past that has driven me towards studying the historical backgrounds of places, dynasties, communities, and families. The popular saying that knowing the past helps in navigating the future is a very apt one, and I believe in it strongly. From the past one can learn a lot that can help in shaping the present and the future, and the past can also teach an individual much about their own self.

I believe that each one of us has an interest in knowing about our past, our family histories, and our roots, although the depth and the degree of this interest varies from person to person. This human curiosity about the past was, and continues to be an integral part of my DNA too, but I was not aware of it as a child. Back in those days, whenever I visited my grandparents, both maternal and paternal, at Ferozepur, I enjoyed listening to them talk about our ancestors and about their own lives. I would ask them questions about their childhood experiences and about the Partition, for both sides of my family had lived through the horrors of that traumatic event. While some of them indulged my curiosity, my grandfather and my father tended to be evasive and avoided these conversations about the past. Perhaps they did not want to be reminded of the pain they had experienced. My grandmother, on the other hand, never shied away from giving me a very honest view of those times and would often tell me about the things she had gone through during the Partition, what her life had been like before and after it. During these trips to Ferozepur, I would often end up visiting various sites of historical importance in and around the city, like the *samadhis* of Sukhdev, Bhagat Singh, and Rajguru, located near the Indo-Pak border, where they were secretly cremated in March 1931, and the famous Saragarhi Chowk that was built in the memory of those soldiers of the Sikh Regiment who had fought a most ferocious battle defending the fort of Saragarhi against an attack by thousands of Pathan raiders in 1897. These visits further fuelled my love for history.

In 2005, I got the chance to visit Pakistan and decided to take my father with me. He had not gone back ever since having fled his home in 1947. We visited a number of places in Pakistan as my father relived his memories — the bungalow the family had lived in in Sheikhupura, and Lahore Fort and Hira Mandi in Lahore. We also went to see Harbansraji Kothi in Civil Lines in Gujranwala, where my father had once lived with his family. At the time of our visit, the house was inhabited by a squadron leader from the Pakistan Air Force, whose family had come from Lucknow during the mass two-way exodus of people that had marked the Partition. He told us that for almost eight or ten years the large kothi had been used as a refugee camp, and that it was only around 1955 that four individual claimants (including his own self) were allotted parts of the house in lieu of the properties they had left behind in India.

The man was gracious enough to let us tour the house from inside, and as we walked through the red-bricked house, I could see that my emotionally reserved father was on the verge of breaking down completely. Before we left, my father went up to the terrace of the house and showed me the high wall over which he had jumped while trying to flee from an angry mob that was intent on destroying the property and setting fire to the house on the night of 18 August 1947. He said that being able to roam around the house after fifty-eight long years was like being on a pilgrimage.

Through all of these experiences, I realised again and again how important it is to know one's past, to understand the situations and the circumstances that have led us to where we are. And also that the things we inherit from our parents and grandparents are things that link us to them. I still have my paternal grandfather's handwritten notes and correspondences, and also his bank passbooks. The picture of his father, Lala Amarnath Uberoi, is also with me. I also have in my possession my maternal grandfather's black *achkan*, which he got tailored and wore when he went to receive the Rai Sahib investiture. Since my height and body shape are quite similar to his, I wear this achnak on occasions. My father's clothes, his files, and other correspondences have all been kept safe and well preserved by the family even though it has been more than fifteen years since his demise. Whenever we go to Bhopal, which is where my parents were settled, we open this treasure trove of an inheritance and it brings back a thousand memories that keep us engaged with our past and with all those to whom we owe our existence.

When I started working on this book, I regretted the fact that I had not undertaken the project sooner. If I had done so, if I had found the time and made the effort to put together this record of our family's history a couple of decades back, I would have had access to my grandparents' and my parents' recollections and remembrances. Their accounts of the past would have been more richer, more detailed, and thus of greater value. While this is something that I will always regret, I went ahead and worked on this record of the Ubercis' family history because I hoped it would become a living, breathing chronicle that will grow and expand with future generations.

I am aware of the fact that because this book focuses on covering the lives of my father Balkrishan Uberoi's ancestors (unto five generations) and of his progeny (unto two generations), it is, as such, narrow in its scope and coverage. But it also does open up the possibility for others from the extended family to pick up the family streams emerging from our common ancestors and their respective spouses. This books then, is essentially the origin pool from where different branches of the family can launch their own family histories and genealogies.

It is with this intent alone that I have collated everything I knew about our family and about what happened in the past into this document, this 'living book' as I see it, for we are what we are, and where we are in life because of those who came before us.

Rajeev Uberoi

Bidhi Chand Lineage Family Tree, hand-drafted by Harbans Raj Uberoi in January 1969

Pedigree Table of ... Uberoi — d. BIDHI CHAND

d. AMARNATH UBEROI — w. Shrimati KIRPA DEVI

Harbans Raj — Balwantdevi Hansraj Rai — Indradevi — Parbhawati — Dhyack — ...

Kewal Krishan — Karta Krishan — Balkrishan — Adarsh Kumari — Swatatar Kumari

Anil Kumar — Neelam — Naini — Sonu — Ashvani — Rajiv — Rashmi — Vivek — Nivedita — Vandana — Kapil ...

Harbans Raj Uberoi
27-1-69.

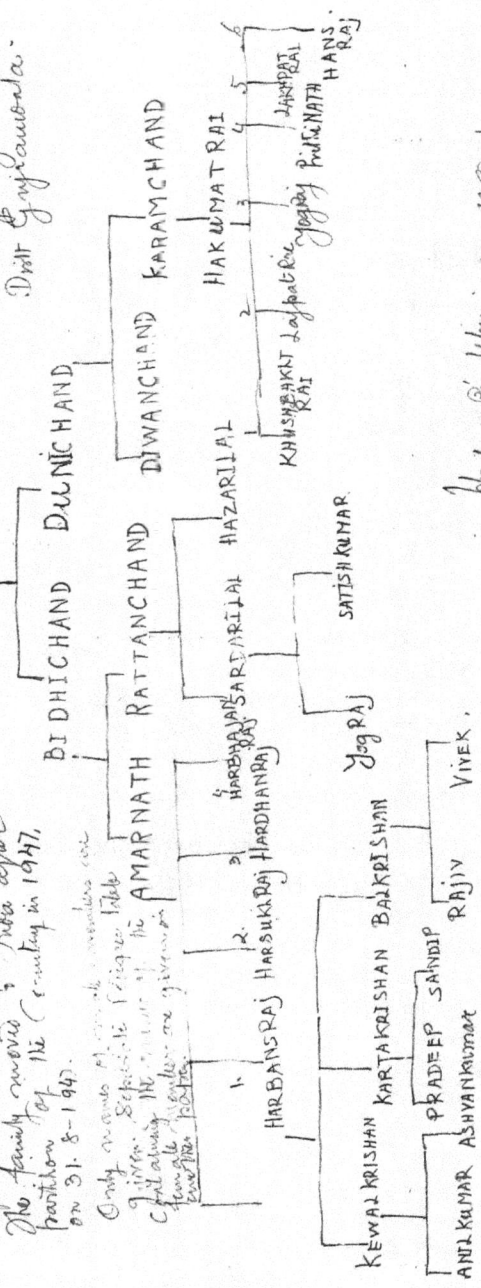

Pedigree Table of the family
of J. Harbans Rai Uberoi Bonbob.
The family moved to India after
partition on the (country in 1947,
partition on 31.8.1947.

Only members of Amarnath members are
given. Separate Pedigree Tables
of the branches of the
Coparcenary. Hereunder are given on
female members are given.

SUDHANA ANAND UBEROI.

SADA ANAND.

Original Home Abar
Y. Ghazakh
Distt Gujranwala.

BIDHICHAND   DULNICHAND

AMARNATH   RATTANCHAND   DIWANCHAND   KARAMCHAND

HARBHAJAN SARDARILAL   HAZARILAL   HAKUMAT RAI

HARBANSRAJ HARSUKHRAJ HARDHANRAJ

YOGRAJ

SATISH KUMAR

KEWAL KRISHAN   KARTAKRISHAN   BALKRISHAN

PRADEEP   SANDIP   RAJIV   VIVEK.

ANILKUMAR   ASHVANKUMAR

KHUSHBAKHT Lajpatrai Yograj Krishnath   JANAKRAJ
RAI

JANAKRAJ   HANS RAJ

1   2   3   4   5   6

Harbans Raj Uberoi Bonbob

Mah Rai Densopore Guj

2.7.1.69.

Sudhana Anand Lineage Family Tree, hand-drafted by Harbans Raj Uberoi in January 1969

GOVERNMENT OF EAST PUNJAB.
(DEPARTMENT OF REHABILITATION)
RESETTLEMENT CARD.

District...*Ferozepore*...

Registration Office No....*Ferozepore city*... Index No..*1765*...

1. Name of head of family...*Lala Harbans Raj Uberoi*...

2. Details of family members.......................*X*

Men-adults	Women-adults	Children (below 10 years)	Infants.
1. Harbans Raj –			*X*
2. Balkrishan			

3. Other particulars; if necessary.........................

Date...*2.2.48*...

Place...*Ferozepore City*...

Signature of Attesting Authority.

Designation *Registration Officer.*

Resettlement card issued by the Government of East Punjab,
Ferozepur, India, to Lala Harbans Raj Uberoi on
2nd February 1948

Chapter 1

A BRIEF HISTORICAL BACKGROUND

❦

The idea of *Bharat Varsh* was born in western India, in the rich plains of what was loosely and historically known as Greater Punjab, a region that was one of the most prosperous regions in the whole world for centuries as it was endowed with fertile alluvial soil, abundant water resources, an excellent climate, a large sea front that facilitated trade and commerce, and a population that was steady, knowledgeable, and skilled in agriculture, trade, commerce, finances, and crafts. Historical excavations of the various Indus Valley Civilisation sites, all of which fall within this area and which are more than 5,000 years old, attest to the prosperity and wealth of Greater Punjab. In fact, the presence of Indus Valley trading seals in civilisations as far away as Mesopotamia suggest that this was a rich region that engaged in brisk trade and commerce. Even prior to this period of recorded history, when the river Saraswati still flowed through present-day Haryana, Rajasthan, and Gujarat, this was the most prosperous landmass globally. Greater Punjab, where my family traces its roots back to, is where the hymns of the Rig Veda were first chanted and where the University of Taxila was established.

But this same richness of resources also brought for this land and its people a great danger in the form of marauding armies of invaders from Central Asia who left nothing but death and destruction in their wake. Where the mighty Himalayas and the Indian Ocean provided a degree of protection to this area, the existence of mountain passes like the Khyber Pass meant that the more persistent of the plunderers could find a passage down into the fertile plains of Punjab, and from there further into the Indian subcontinent. Punjab was, in other words, a gateway into the subcontinent. So it was that this land was looted and wars were fought along the banks of its rivers again and again. The famous war between Alexander the Great and Porus, a war which ended in the crushing defeat of Alexander's army, was fought here for instance. The fierce battle between the Pandavas and the Kauravas, as described in the Mahabharata, was fought here too. While most of these invaders went back to their respective homelands after plundering the resources of Punjab, it was with the establishment of the Mughal empire in India around the early 16th century that the nature of governance and rule in the region underwent a change with the invaders now staying back to consolidate their stronghold and expand their control. Later, as the Mughal hold weakened, Raja Ranjit Singh, also known as the Lion of Punjab, successfully set up the Khalsa Raj in the region. At the peak of his power, his domain stretched from Afghanistan in the northwest to the Sutlej River in the east and from Kashmir in the north to the Thar desert in the south. Within a few years of his death in 1839, however, the Sikh kingdom that he had carved out collapsed and the British successfully annexed Punjab after the Battle of Lahore in 1848-49.

With the British conquest of Punjab began a new chapter in the history of the region. Its resources were now co-opted into the grand imperial project of creating an empire in India. The British ruthlessly exploited the human and material resources of Punjab during their numerous expansionist campaigns like the Anglo-Afghan Wars and the First World War. Punjab actually provided the largest contingent of soldiers (comprising Muslims, Hindus, and Sikhs, with Sikhs being in the majority) for the British army as compared to all other native contingents. The British government worked on developing the existing infrastructure of the region, for instance the expansion of the network of canals, to further agricultural production and use it to advance their expansionary aspirations.

Apart from these forced economic and political changes that often demolished the culture and heritage of Punjab and left its people in penury, another very critical change that took place was the religious persecution of the local inhabitants, predominantly followers of the Hindu religion, by those in power and the resultant change in the social dynamics of the land. There were, for example, large scale conversions to Islam in the period before the establishment of the Khalsa Raj. Later, as the British strengthened their rule and there was an increase in missionary presence in the region, there were conversions to Christianity as well. Though the instances of religious conversion were spread across the social structure of Punjab, it was primarily the poorer working class to which the converts belonged to. There were economic compulsions, the expectation of a better life under the new rulers, and the fear of persecution leading to death which prompted these conversions to Islam, Christianity, and even Sikhism. But what all these conversions had in common was the long-term impact they had on the social and cultural fabric of the area, with the population getting increasingly fragmented and divided. And it was not just the people who were getting divided. The land too, was getting divided, and what was once Greater Punjab is now a landmass split into many countries— India, Pakistan, Afghanistan, and then further into states like, Sind, Pakistan Punjab, Indian Punjab, Haryana, and Himachal Pradesh.

In terms of social stratification, the typical Hindu *varna* (caste) system did exist in the region, with menial workers being considered to be the lower class, followed by semi-skilled workers who worked as artisans, masons, etc., traders who were by and large Hindu, and finally, those who provided services in the administration and in the military. The *brahman* community in Punjab, while technically being at the top of the varna structure, were not very well off and their role was limited to providing religious and educational services. Overall though, the people of Punjab were mainly skilled agriculturists who were resilient in the face of unwanted upheavals and crises.

While there is a long history of religious conversion in Punjab, there were some sets of people who resisted conversion and continued to pursued their religious beliefs. These included people belonging to the warrior class, administrators, and those engaged in trade and commerce. The Khatris historically belonged to the first group and because they were well established and economically better off than most others, they were able to climb up the social hierarchy. They played an important role during the Mughals' rule of Punjab, during Raja Ranjit Singh's reign, and even during the days of the British, going on to occupy positions of power as administrators, lawyers, doctors, and businessmen. They also played an extremely critical role in the trans-regional trade of Punjab, selling cloth and various other items from the Indian subcontinent and setting up trading and moneylending links with places like Isfahan (Iran).

The Uberois/Oberois/Obhrais are Khatris who can trace their roots back to the areas of Sialkot, Gujranwala, Gujarat (Punjab), and Peshawar in modern-day Pakistan. They were educated landowners and traders, and they also worked in various capacities in the administration both during the Khalsa Raj and under the British. My family, in particular, comes from the small village of Garjakh, located a few miles from Gujranwala, which is now a district in Pakistan, but which used to be the capital of the Khalsa Raj during the initial days of its existence. It is to Garjakh that we shall go back to start unfolding the story of how the Uberoi family came to where it is today.

Chapter 2

GARJAKH

W estern Punjab was a pastoral region endowed with very fertile land and abundant water resources. It was the land of five rivers— Indus, Chenab, Beas, Sutlej, and Jhelum—and that was also what gave it its name: Punjab, 'punj' meaning five and 'aab' meaning water. It is here, in this region, and more specifically the areas of Sialkot, Gujranwal, Gujarat, and Peshawar, that the story of the Uberois starts from. Belonging to the prominent Khatri caste, the Uberois were primarily educated landowners and traders, and also worked in various capacities in the administration, both during the days of the Khalsa Raj and the British era.

The Uberoi family traces its roots back to the small village of Garjakh, located a few miles from Gujranwala, which is now a district in Pakistan, but which used to be the capital of the Khalsa Raj during the initial days of its existence.

Situated between the rivers Ravi and Churah and irrigated by their tributaries, Garjakh was blessed with very fertile land and was therefore a predominantly agricultural economy with most of its people engaged in agriculture, and in dairy and poultry farming. Its proximity to Gujranwala ensured that there was a steady demand for its agricultural produce in the markets of the town. When the British established their rule over Punjab, this hamlet had a population of less than 2,000 people spread across a hundred odd households. It had a school that ran classes upto the eighth standard with the medium of instruction being Urdu and Gurmukhi. There was a police outpost, but no medical facilities. The village had two temples and a single mosque.

The social composition of the village was dominated by Muslim families who worked as farmhands, water carriers, butchers, and metal workers. Most of the land and the businesses in the village were owned by Sikh and Hindu families. The Hindu businessmen, or the Khatris, ran small grocery shops, engaged in the wholesale trade of grains, and also offered moneylending services. The more well-to-do Hindus were addressed as *shahji* or *lalaji*, while the Sikhs were addressed as *sardar bahadur*, and the Muslims were called *karindas*. What is interesting to note here is the fact that while the West Punjab region had been under Muslim rule for many centuries, and the land should have logically been owned by the Pathans and the Afghans, it was not so. In 1774, when Charat Singh, the grandfather of Ranjit Singh, defeated the local Gujjars, he confiscated their lands and gave all of it to his own faithful followers. Thus, even though Muslims were in a numerical majority in the region, the ownership and the control of all the land and the wealth rested in the hands of the Sikhs and the Hindus.

Most of the houses in Garjakh were *kutcha* houses built with mud and topped with a thatched roof. While the wealthy owned a couple of wells, the communal village well was the only source of drinking water for the less privileged of Garjakh, especially the Muslims.

Like other Khatris, the Uberois of Garjakh owned a lot of land and traded in agricultural produce, while also engaging in the moneylending business. In the early 19th century, the family owned a large three-storeyed haveli, one of the only five or six pucca houses in Garjakh. The patriarch of the family was Sudhana Nand Uberoi, who had two sons — Lala Bidhi Chand Uberoi and Lala Dhuni Chand Uberoi. While not much is known about the younger son Dhuni Chand and his family, the elder son, Bidhi Chand, who was my great great grandfather, was educated in a Khalsa school in Gujranwala. He would walk three miles everyday to attend school, and was one of the brighter students. By the time he completed his matriculation, the British government, having annexed Punjab, was in the process of setting up an administrative structure in Gujranwala, which had been given the status of a district in 1853-54. They set up a revenue department in the town and began recruiting educated youth from the region to staff this new department. With his knowledge of the area and his good grades, Bidhi Chand was able to join the newly created revenue service. He served the British government for more than twenty-eight years and retired as an assistant deputy collector.

Lala Bidhi Chand's work took him all over North-West Punjab as he steadily made his way up the revenue department hierarchy. During this period, while most of the family continued living in the village, some members, like his wife, children, and a few of his siblings, moved to a house that the family built in the town of Gujranwala, for it offered easier access to better educational facilities for the children. The cost of living in Gujranwala was not very high as most of the grocery items and the agricultural produce required by the household were sent from the village.

While Gujranwala had been a pretty well-organised town even during the days of the Khalsa Raj, it developed rather rapidly under the British who wanted to showcase their commitment to the area and the community by encouraging the town's growth and expansion. Under the Sikh administration, Gujranwala had seen the construction of numerous gardens, gurdwaras, large havelis, schools, and canals. The British now built on this existing infrastructural framework — they developed and expanded the Grand Trunk Road that had originally been built by Sher Shah Suri from Peshawar to New Delhi in the 15th century. A railway line was laid in 1863. A new European colony was established. Churches and more schools were set up as well, and the local school was upgraded to a college. Roads and canals were built too, to improve connectivity and irrigation, all of which had a direct bearing on the revenue-generating potential of the region.

British efforts to improve the infrastructure of Gujranwala resulted in the town experiencing a very fast pace of economic growth and development. The people became better off in general and the landed gentry and the educated became wealthier. With better revenue laws, administrative structures, and law and order situation, Gujranwala flourished. By moving his family to Gujranwala, Lala Bidhi Chand had ensured that his progeny and his siblings would have access to better education and a much improved quality of life.

This move from a rural to an urban environment not only gave Bidhi Chand's family the opportunity to be better educated, but it also ignited in them the desire to progress in life. As a result, like most other urban, wealthy Hindus of the region, they found themselves greatly influenced by the teachings of Swami Dayanand Saraswati, the founder of Arya Samaj. The Arya Samaj essentially subscribed to Vedic philosophy and stood against many of the evils that were then prevalent in society, like child marriage, untouchability, prohibitions against the remarriage of widows and against the education of girls, idol worship, excessive spending on religious ceremonies, etc. In encouraging such radical ideas as the education of girls and the remarriage of widows, the Arya Samaj had a massive impact on the social structure of Punjab, and Bidhi Chand, with his educated progressive mindset, took an active part in the affairs of the Arya Samaj. This meant that apart from the boys, all the girls in the family were given a good education too—they were sent to the local village school and instructed in religious literature— and that the family, as a whole, had a more modern and progressive outlook that enabled them to keep up with the times.

After his retirement from the revenue department, Lala Bidhi Chand returned to Garjakh and settled there after having been away from the village for almost twenty years. He began looking after the family land and constructed a large three-storey pucca house in the village. Well-built and fair complexioned, this beloved patriarch of the family could often be found walking slowly along the village roads, dressed in his *themat*, a long cloth tied around the waist, and a kurta, with a large shawl, traditionally called the *dorshalla*, wrapped around his body to keep out the early morning cold. He would carry with him a walking stick, not because he needed one, but because it came in handy to keep the stray dogs away. Those who passed him by would greet him with respect, calling him *shahji*.

In these later years, Bidhi Chand mostly kept himself restricted to his village surroundings. He devoted his time to various social activities in the village and the Arya Samaj. His children were all married and well-settled by now. His elder son was practising law in Gujranwala. One of his younger sons had started his own business by opening a provision store in the village. Along with this, he also lent money to those who needed it as the village had very few wealthy families and a large percentage of the population consisted of impoverished Muslim and lower-class Hindu families. His daughters also lived in and around the village with their individual families. With his pension coming in regularly and because of the escalation in the value of land in Garjakh, Lala Bidhi Chand led a very comfortable post-retirement life. He lived till the ripe old age of seventy, and died peacefully in his village home, secure in the knowledge that everything was in order in his family.

If one were to compare the Garjakh of today with what it was during Lala Bidhi Chand's time, it will be easy to see that the village has undergone what can only be described as a sea change. Garjakh, the village of my great great grandfather's time does not exist anymore. It has now become a part of the sprawling city of Gujranwala. There are malls here and numerous schools too. Paved roads have been laid. A brand new police station has been established to support the growing population. Old kutcha buildings have been replaced with new concrete ones. This is, of course, the story everywhere, with everything old being largely seen as redundant and irrelevant. But in the case of the Uberois of Garjakh, it would bode us well to always remember that it was Lala Bidhi Chand's foresight and open-mindedness that instilled in his children a sense of culture and a value system that would stand them in good stead as they moved through their lives and carried the family line ahead.

Chapter 3

GUJRANWALA

It is a well-established truth that in most families there is that one individual who plays the role of a game-changer and opens the doors for the family's growth and development in ways that might not have been imagined as being otherwise possible. Such a person is far-sighted, intelligent, and hard-working. And if all other external factors align, they can easily help push the family up to higher levels of success and achievements. Lala Bidhi Chand's eldest son, Amarnath, was just such a person. He was intelligent and bright, and excelled in his studies both at school and then in college. After his graduation, when Amarnath decided to study law, Lala Bidhi Chand supported his decision. There was no reason for him not to do so. In the thirty years that the British had been in charge of Punjab, they had established a robust revenue and

judicial system. Macaulay had codified the Indian Penal
Code in 1872. A high court had been established at Lahore,
along with the Government Law College. There were
district courts that had started functioning in Gujranwala,
and being a rich agricultural belt, the number of both civil
and criminal cases had increased within a short period of
time, which translated into a growing demand for lawyers
who were trained in the British legal system. The legal
profession was, quite simply put, doing very well in the
region.

Amarnath enrolled himself in the Government Law
College in Lahore to get his law degree. His stay in the city
exposed him not just to the complexities and nuances of
English law, but also to the British way of life. Lahore was,
after all, a prosperous town with a flourishing European
population. It was also the seat of the governor's office. In
Lahore, Amarnath acquired a strongly Western taste when
it came to his lifestyle. During this period, he also met and
interacted with stalwarts like Saifuddin Kitchlew and Lala
Lajpat Rai, who were also studying law. The relationships
he built during his years as a law student in Lahore and
the contacts he made would help him a lot in the years
ahead, especially because while the actual seat of English
power in India was the city of Calcutta in the east, with the
British intent on setting up an equally strong and powerful
administrative structure in Punjab, the scope for individual
expansion and success in the region was immense.

Between the 1860s and the 1890s, the social and
religious renaissance that was sweeping through Punjab
did not leave Amarnath untouched. Apart from acquiring

a decidedly Western outlook, he also took active part in student activities and politics, and following in his father's footsteps, became an active member of the Arya Samaj, keeping company with people like Swami Shradhanand, who took over the mantle of the Arya Samaj after the demise of its founder. Amarnath would go on to build an Arya Samaj temple in Gujranwala and would also organise regular discourses for the followers of the Samaj. All these seemingly diverse influences came together to enable Amarnath to evolve into a leader who would be instrumental in bringing change to Gujranwala.

After acquiring his law degree in Lahore, Amarnath came back to Gujranwala to start his practise in the district court. He also registered himself with the Lahore High Court Bar as a junior lawyer. At this point in time, the district courts in Punjab were hungry for good lawyers, especially those trained in English law. While some lawyers had moved from Calcutta to Punjab when the British had started setting up their law courts in the region, there were still not enough lawyers to meet the increasing caseload, and more importantly, the higher judiciary was entirely filled with Englishmen. Also, most of the legal professionals who were already practising law in Punjab were all trained in the Islamic system of law, which had been the law of the land until then. Most of them did not deem it necessary to study and familiarise themselves with the ways of English law. As a result, when Amarnath set up his legal practise in Gujranwala, lawyers like him were a rarity and he was able to successfully establish himself within a very short period of time. He became a leading lawyer while he was still in his early forties and was among the few lawyers who represented local clients in appeals in the high court in Lahore. Not only that, Amarnath also became the president of the District Bar Association within a couple of years, which was not surprising given the fact that he was well-respected by everyone, including the Europeans who filled the ranks of the higher judiciary. He built his chamber near the court and had a very busy schedule. He had a number of apprentices and junior lawyers working for him, helping him prepare the suits while he made regular appearances in the Lahore High Court. Everyday, he would reach his chamber by 11 a.m. and prepare for the cases listed for the day with the junior lawyers and then go to the court for the hearings. He would return to his chamber by late afternoon, give directions to his apprentices about preparing for the next day's caseload, and then go home. Such was his popularity that increasingly, his social circle included people who were well-placed within the administrative and judicial services and also those who were recognised as being amongst the wealthiest of landowners and businessmen in Gujranwala.

On the home front, his young family was growing — his firstborn, Harbans Raj Uberoi, was born on 01 January 1896 in Gujranwala. In the years that followed, Lala Amarnath had three more sons and four daughters, all of whom were raised very well and given good educations. While the sons were educated in local schools and then sent to Lahore for their graduation, the girls, in keeping with prevalent traditions, were not sent to colleges in other towns that would take them away from the protective influence of their parents and were, instead, sent to a local college. Again, in keeping with tradition, the girls were all married off when they were in their late teens and the boys were married when they were in their early twenties. Although the family was based entirely in Gujranwala, Amarnath often went to Garjakh to provide support to his father and the extended family. He bought a tonga which helped him reduce the amount of time it took him to commute to Garjakh. With his legal practise doing so well, Amarnath was able to help his father in getting all his sisters married and in educating his brothers. Just like his father had done before him, Amarnath took good care of the whole family.

As the Uberoi family's fortunes grew richer, in the background, the social and political atmosphere in Punjab was beginning to roil and rumble. While the establishment of the British government in the region had brought with it a degree of religious freedom for the people, what it also brought with it was an awareness of the world beyond. In the rural areas of Punjab, for example, the last quarter of the last century had seen substantial recruitment of soldiers by the British Indian Army. When these soldiers came back home, they brought with them news of everything that was happening in the outside world, thus exposing their families and villages to a growing body of knowledge and awareness about their rights. People began to see the British government for what it actually was and not what they had been led to believe. They began to recognise the various ways in which they were being exploited and suppressed in their own land. It was in this politically charged atmosphere that the Indian National Congress (INC) and later the Indian Muslim League were founded. Within ten years of its existence, the INC had a strong base in Punjab, and

Gujranwala, which was now counted amongst the larger towns of the region, had an active INC presence. While a major percentage of the party's membership consisted of impoverished Muslims, Hindus, and Sikhs who had been newly converted to Christianity by the missionaries, in Gujranwala, the INC also attracted the wealthier Sikh and Hindu families into its ranks. Among them, taking a very active part in its proceedings was Amarnath. He built a very strong relationship with the party's state level leaders like Lala Lajpat Rai and Saifuddin Kitchlew, and often frequented Lahore for party meetings. When the INC's annual conference was hosted by the Punjab chapter in Amritsar in 1919, Amarnath played an important role in organising the conference and even appears in the photographs taken on that occasion, standing beside senior leaders like Motilal Nehru and Madan Mohan Malaviya. Because of his fervour and his devotion to the cause, Amarnath not only came to the forefront of party affairs, but he also rose to become the president of the Gujranwala chapter of the INC.

The second decade of the twentieth century was full of turmoil all across the world. In India too, tensions were simmering under the surface. When the First World War broke out in 1914, even though India was not directly involved in the war, it was dragged into the conflict because Indian resources, from food grains and cotton cloth to money and soldiers, were used aggressively by the British government to fund its war requirements. In fact, the British Indian Army fought in many battlefields spread across France, Italy, North Africa, and other parts of the European continent. Rulers of many Indian princely states too funded the British war efforts and put their armies and coffers at the disposal of the British.

As the war dragged on, however, the grim realities of conflict became apparent to the Indian public. There was galloping inflation across the land on account of the Indian economy being drained of its resources to fight the war, and this drain was especially harmful for the poor and the downtrodden. To add fuel to the fire, the Indian soldiers returning from the war were not treated well by the British government, and as a majority of them were from Punjab, public discontent in the region thickened. Large-scale political rallies began to be organised all across Punjab, with Lahore as the epicentre of all this political activity. The Indian National Congress led many of these political rallies and emerged very clearly as the people's chosen representative when it came to negotiating for change with the British government. The fact that after the First World War ended, the global political fabric underwent a sea change with monarchies being replaced by democratic, socialist, and communist regimes—the fall of the Tsarist monarchy in Russia being the most spectacular example of such a regime change—meant that these changes also had a massive impact on the political atmosphere in India. The sense of nationalism amongst the people of India grew stronger in the post-war period, more so in Punjab, since it was a more politically active region when compared to other areas.

In February 1919, a couple of months before the First World War officially ended with the signing of the Treaty of Versailles, the British government, in a preventive move to stem the growing tide of political discontent in India, passed the Rowlatt Act which granted it sweeping powers to try political cases without conducting a due trial in the presence of a jury. In effect, it allowed the state to arrest anyone and put them in jail if they were perceived as a threat to the state. Quite obviously, the passage of this act led to massive resentment among the people and protests were organised all over the country. In Punjab, it was the intelligentsia that led these protests with prominent lawyers like Lala Lajpat Rai and Saifuddin Kitchlew at the forefront of the large-scale demonstrations that took place in Lahore, Kasur, Amritsar, Peshawar, and Gujranwala. Amarnath too, was a part of these largely peaceful gatherings.

Things however came to a head on 13 April 1919 in Amritsar where thousands of people had gathered in Jallianwala Bagh, an open space near the Harmandir Sahib Gurdwara, to celebrate *baisakhi*, a festival which marks the beginning of the new year in Punjab after the crops have been harvested. There were children, women, and men who were gathered there in peaceful celebration in spite of there being a government ban in place against public gatherings. Jallianwala Bagh had just one gate for entry and exit and it was surrounded with high wall on all sides. On receiving news of the public gathering, General Reginald Dyer, the man appointed by the British government to maintain the law and order situation in Amritsar, marched to Jallianwala Bagh with his soldiers, sealed off the single exit point, and ordered his men to indiscriminately shoot at the unarmed men, women, and children gathered within. His orders left hundreds of innocent civilians dead and thousands injured.

Even as martial law was imposed on Punjab, news of this gruesome incident spread like wild fire across the whole of India. There were widespread demonstrations in many cities and towns which, in spite of tempers running high, were still mostly peaceful.

In Gujranwala, meanwhile, although there had been *hartals* that had been organised by the local political leaders, the law and order situation had mostly been under control. Lala Amarnath, who was the president of the District Congress Committee, had had discussions with both the district deputy commissioner and the district superintendent of police to assure them that in spite of the protests taking place in the town, there would be no violence. On 6 April, complete hartal was observed in Gujranwala, and the Congress leaders submitted a memorandum of their demands to the district administration while also observing a fast. Things remained peaceful in Gujranwala until after 13 April, Baisakhi day, when news of the massacre in Amritsar first started trickling in. By the next day, 14 April, there were stories and rumours circulating about the public floggings and humiliations that were being meted out to people in Amritsar. It was also rumoured that a dead calf had been hung up on one of the railways bridges just outside Gujranwala. The news of the Jallianwala Bagh tragedy had already incensed the people in the city, and this last rumour about the dead calf only fanned the flames of their anger further. It might have been a rumour that was spread deliberately to rouse the Hindu population and create a divide between them and the Muslims. Fortunately though, the ploy did not work and both the communities came out together in protest against what had happened in Jallianwala Bagh. They gathered in a large crowd late in the afternoon in the centre of the town near the Ghanta Ghar, the clock tower. Various leaders of the Gujranwala chapter of the INC made speeches against the Rowlatt Act and the massacre in Jallianwala Bagh, and once the political speeches were over, it was decided that a memorandum should be submitted immediately to the deputy commissioner of police. With this intent, the crowd started marching towards the office of the district commissioner, and leading this crowd was Amarnath.

As they moved towards the DC's office, the number of people in the procession started to swell and people began to get restless. It is very likely that there were some people in the crowd who wanted to use violence to express their anger. When they were crossing the railway station, some of these people suddenly started pelting the station building with stones. All hell broke loose, and within a matter of a few minutes things had escalated beyond imagination. There were suddenly people in the crowd who were carrying torches and setting the building on fire. Even as Amarnath and the other Congress leaders watched aghast and tried to control the situation, the people now started moving towards the town's European settlement. A church and some of the bungalows of government officials were looted and ransacked.

By now, news of the angry mob had reached not just the deputy commissioner of police but also the governor's office in Lahore. Even as the mob surged towards his office, the DC realised that controlling it was beyond the capacity of the local police force, especially since most of the members of the police force were all residents of

Gujranwala itself and might, therefore, be reluctant to go against their brethren. He sent an immediate SOS to Lahore, asking for additional forces and help to regain control of the situation.

Gujranwala is about 50 miles north-west of Lahore. It would have taken a couple of hours for the governor's office to mobilise the necessary number of men and resources and then send them to the burning city. Added to this was the fact that there were widespread demonstrations happening in Lahore itself, and it would not have been wise to remove forces from the city and send them elsewhere. In this precariously volatile situation, the governor of Punjab ordered the use of an aeroplane mounted with a machine gun to be sent to Gujranwala to lend air support to its police force and help it control the crowd.

It took about an hour for a single-engine Tiger Moth aircraft mounted with a machine gun to fly from Lahore to Gujranwala, and once it reached the town and began showering bullets on the unarmed crowd on the ground, it created bedlam as the crowd ran helter-skelter to save their lives. There was no cover for them to hide under. At the end of about fifteen minutes of firing, when the aircraft finally left, the crowd had disbursed entirely, leaving many dead and grievously injured lying on the ground. It must be noted here that although this incident has never been highlighted in the history of the period, this was the first instance of a state sanctioning the use of air weaponry against unarmed civilians.

Meanwhile, by now, help from the neighbouring towns of Wazirabad and Aminabad had also reached

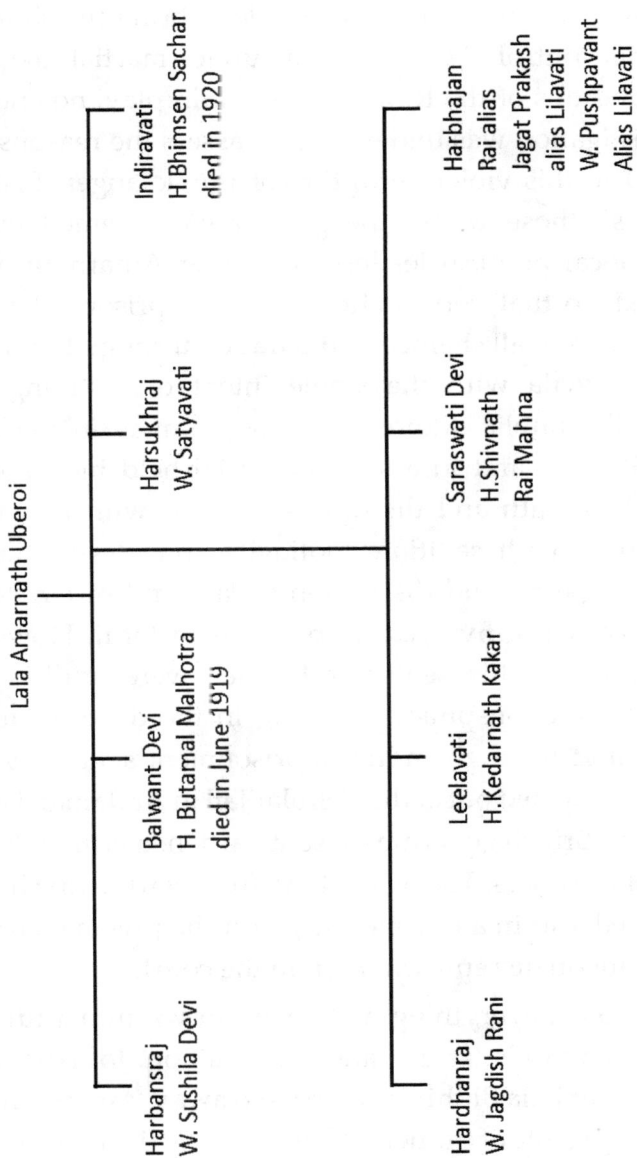

Lala Amarnath Uberoi

Harbansraj
W. Sushila Devi

Balwant Devi
H. Butamal Malhotra
died in June 1919

Harsukhraj
W. Satyavati

Indiravati
H.Bhimsen Sachar
died in 1920

Hardhanraj
W. Jagdish Rani

Leelavati
H.Kedarnath Kakar

Saraswati Devi
H.Shivnath
Rai Mahna

Harbhajan
Rai alias
Jagat Prakash
alias Lilavati
W. Pushpavant
Alias Lilavati

Gujranwala, and with this additional backup supporting them, the local police force was able to bring the situation under its control. As Punjab was under martial law with the provisions of the Rowlatt Act still in play, no enquiry or investigation was undertaken to assess the reasons that had led to this violent eruption of public anger. Instead, to punish those whom the government deemed guilty, all the local political leaders, including Amarnath, were rounded up that very night and put in prison. The next day, they were all chained and paraded through the streets of Gujranwala with the single intent of instilling fear among the public. More arrests were made in the days that followed, and in a summary trial held by a special court, Amarnath and the others arrested with him were all charged with sedition, looting, arson, destruction of public property, and disruption of law and order. Many were awarded a five-year imprisonment term. However, Amarnath and his senior colleagues were additionally charged with conspiracy resulting in the death of many people, and were given life imprisonment sentences that were to be carried out at the Cellular Jail in Andaman Island where the British government sent hardened criminals and political prisoners. The whole trial, from start to finish, was completed within a few months, with the prisoners barely getting adequate representation in the court.

At home, everything had been thrown into a turmoil with Amarnath's arrest and deportation to Andaman Island. After Lala Bidhi Chand passed away, Amarnath had assumed the role of the head of the family. His siblings were all settled, but he still played the important role of guiding them and helping them out. His own family consisted of eight children between the ages of ten and twenty-two. With him behind the bars, not only had Amarnath's law practice taken a nosedive, but his entire family was left floundering. His eldest son, Harbansraj, having recently completed his law degree from the Government Law College in Lahore, had just started working in Amarnath's chambers along with his friend Bhimsen Sachar. Now, with Amarnath imprisoned, the responsibility of taking care of the family and of fighting Amarnath's court case fell on the two young men.

The two youngsters worked hard to keep the legal practice afloat so that the family could survive this terrible ordeal. But it wasn't an easy task. Under British laws, the properties of any person found guilty of sedition are confiscated, and this became the sword of Damocles for the family, threatening its very survival. The only glimmer of hope during these testing times was the fact that the senior leaders of the Indian National Congress provided great support to the family. They filed an appeal on Amarnath's behalf in the Lahore High Court and the case was argued by Mohan Das Karamchand Gandhi himself, having just returned to India from South Africa.

The hearing went on for more than a year, with both Harbans Rajand Bhimsen Sachar helping the battery of senior lawyers working on the case. Very convincing arguments were put forth in Amarnath's defence. By now, things had settled in Punjab as there had been a global uproar against the Jallianwala Bagh massacre. The Rowlatt Act had been withdrawn and General Dyer had also been sent back to England. It seemed that things could, very possibly, swing in Amarnath's favour. Finally, when the judgment was delivered in 1920, the life imprisonment sentence that had been awarded to Amarnath by the special court was condoned as the government could not prove either the presence of criminal intent or that there had been a conspiracy afoot. What was proved beyond doubt was the fact that the events that had transpired in Gujranwala were a result of mob frenzy and not a planned act against the state.

However, in a final move to save its face, the court asked Amarnath to submit a written apology for his role in the episode. His properties were released, but the high court banned him from practicing law and appearing in any court under its jurisdiction. Furthermore, he was disbarred from taking part in any political activities in the region.

It had, in the end, taken two long years for Amarnath to be released from prison. Although his release came as a great respite for the family, Amarnath himself did not keep in good health in the years after his release. Being restricted from taking part in political activities and from practising law, both of which were his passions, took a great mental toll on him. Slowly, however, as he started settling back into the new routines of his life, he turned his attention to the task of settling his family. Harbans Raj was already married to Sushila Devi. Amarnath now approached Bhimsen Sachar with a proposal of marriage with his eldest daughter. After a bit of initial hesitation, Bhimsen agreed to get married to Amarnath's eldest daughter. A little after that, Amarnath's second daughter, Balwant, was married to Dr Kapoor, a doctor working in the Malaria Eradication Mission. His second son, Harsukhraj, was studying in Khalsa College in Gujranwala, while the remaining two,

Hardhanraj and Harpratap were still in school. The two younger daughters, Saraswati and Leelawati, were also coming of age. But before they could be married off, there was a tragedy in the family. Bhimsen's wife, the eldest daughter of the family, died within a couple of months of her marriage. Her sudden death was a massive shock for the entire family. They were still coming out of all the pain and suffering they had been through in the years when Amarnath had been imprisoned. The death of a beloved daughter came as a harsh blow, but such was the cruelty of fate. After his wife's death, Bhimsen Sachar decided to move to Lahore to establish himself there. Eventually, he would go on to remarry and build another family.

Even as the family was struggling to come to terms with the tragedy, another one struck it down like a bolt of lightening. Dr Kapoor died an untimely death while travelling to Nagpur, and his widow Balwant came back to live with her parents with a small daughter, not more than a couple of years old, in tow. Somehow though, the family managed to move forward in spite of these tragedies. The fact that they were all together in their grief was, in all likelihood, the greatest source of their strength.

Amarnath's two remaining daughters were soon married off as well. Saraswati was married to Mr Mohna, who was a lawyer as well, and the youngest, Leelawati, was married to Mr Kedarnath Kakar, who belonged to a well-respected landed family of Ferozepur.

Amarnath now led a largely retired life, splitting his time between Garjakh and Gujranwala. He would visit his chamber sometimes to offer advice to Harbans Raj and his clients. Bhimsen Sachar's move to Lahore had been a setback to the legal practise that Amarnath had set up, and things were further aggravated by the government's decision to bifurcate Gujranwala into two districts, Sheikhupura and Gujranwala, for administrative purposes. Many cases were transferred to the district court that was being set up in Sheikhupura, and for a good two or three years, Harbans Raj kept travelling between Gujranwala and Sheikhupura for work, until he eventually moved his work and family to Sheikhupura.

It took time, but things did stabilise for the Uberoi family. Harsukhraj completed his graduation and got a job with the newly incorporated nationalist-sponsored Punjab National Bank. Harpratap, not having completed his schooling, devoted himself to tilling the land that the family owned at Garjakh, and Hardhanraj, the youngest son, continued pursuing his education at Lahore. While being unable to actively participate in politics, Amarnath continued to keep in regular touch with his friends in the Indian National Congress. However, he kept a very low profile because he was very mindful of the fact that any apparent association with him could have an adverse impact on his friends in the Congress and on their political agenda. These were important years for the Indian national movement, and it would have been foolhardy for both Amarnath and his friends in the Congress to take any unnecessary risks that could potentially derail the pace of the national movement. By now, Lala Lajpat Rai had emerged as a national-level leader. With the idea of *swaraj* gaining momentum in the country, he had helped in the establishment of nationalist enterprises like the Punjab National Bank and the Sunlight Insurance Company. The setting up of organisations like these was an absolute game changer for they marked the first steps towards Indians reclaiming their economic independence.

Amarnath now started devoting more time to the pursuit of religious activities and began working closely with Swami Shradhanand, the leader of the Arya Samaj. He continued with his social work for a long long time, and every once in a while, he would visit Lahore to meet his old friends and colleagues. He was always accompanied by Harbans Raj on these trips.

As the years passed, Amarnath became increasingly weak and frail, although the spark of fire in him never really banked. He took to spending more and more time in Sheikhupura to be with his family — two of his children had shifted to Sheikhupura with their entire families, and two of his sons were based in Lahore, which was only two hours away from Sheikhupura — and spend his later years in the warmth of familial love and comfort. He lived till the ripe old age of seventy, and passed away just a few years before the outbreak of the Second World War. My father, Balkrishan Uberoi, must have been about ten years old at the time of Lala Amarnath's death. He has very vivid memories of returning to Gujranwala for his grandfather's final rites, and says that the entire family was there to bid farewell to the departed soul. Also present at the funeral were senior leaders of the Congress and the Arya Samaj, who paid glowing tributes to the work that Lala Amarnath had done throughout his life.

Like his father before him, Lala Amarnath Uberoi's life is a perfect example of how with the right education and moral upbringing, a person can not only pave the way for great success in his or her life, but also ensure that the benefits of a better life are accessible to the rest of their families as well. Not only did Lala Amarnath set up a flourishing legal practise in Gujranwala, but he also devoted his life to the political awakening of the country and to various social activities in Gujranwala, and through it all, he carried forward his father's legacy while also establishing his own.

Chapter 4

SHEIKHUPURA

The next chapter in the history of the Uberoi family began with Harbans Raj moving his family to Sheikhupura where he had started spending more and more time because of work. According to documentary evidence, the foundation of Sheikhupura was laid by Emperor Jahangir, also known as Sheikhu, in 1607 CE, when he visited the region to hunt deer. Earlier records show that this place was called Jehangirpura, and that it was established near the old town of Jandiala Sher Khan which was about 40 kilometres away from Lahore. A fort was built in Sheikhupura by the Mughals, but it fell into disuse as their power and glory declined, and in the period before the Khalsa Raj was established in Punjab, the Sheikhupura fort served as a hiding place for bandits, especially for a dacoit named Lehara Singh. However, under the Khalsa Raj, the Sheikhupura fort became a very important fort. Maharaja Ranjit Singh granted this fort as a jagir to his wife Datar Kaur, who was also known as Mai Nakkin, and she got a haveli built in the Kangra style of architecture within the fort premises. The last famous inhabitant of the fort was Rani Jindan, the mother of Maharaja Duleep Singh, the last emperor of the Sikh Empire, who lived here till she was banished from Punjab in 1848.

Under the British, Sheikhupura lost some of its glory and importance as it was made a part of the Gujranwala district. But in the 1920s, the British decided it would make better administrative sense to give Sheikhupura the designation of a district headquarter, and post this move, the town regained its lost glory, reclaiming immense volumes of trade and commerce from Gujranwala as the balance of administrative power shifted in its favour. The town's rich history and its proximity to Lahore also helped. As did the fact that it was located in a very fertile area of Punjab that was irrigated by an excellent system of rivers and canals. Sheikhupura was a huge source of grains, vegetables, and other edible items for the city of Lahore. After it was made a district, the amount of government investment in the town's economy increased, with the result that numerous agro-based industries were established here and trade and commerce flourished. New schools and hospitals were also built in the town and a new railway line was laid from Lahore to Hafizabad, with a crossing at Sheikhupura. With better infrastructure and connectivity came the benefits of all-round economic growth and development. By the time Harbans Raj shifted

Dr Vinod Chandar Nanda and Shashi Nanda

Satish Uberoi, Adarsh Loomba and Swatantra Chopra, Ferozepur

The Uberoi daughters-in-law — Sharda, Satish and Sanjokta

Indu Vinayak's *doli* ceremony, during her wedding with Jitender Krishan Puri. Seen here with her brother and Rajeev's maternal uncle, Ramesh Chander Vinayak

Ganeshilal Sondhi and Saroj Sondhi

4-year old Rajeev with his parents, Balkrishan and Satish Bala

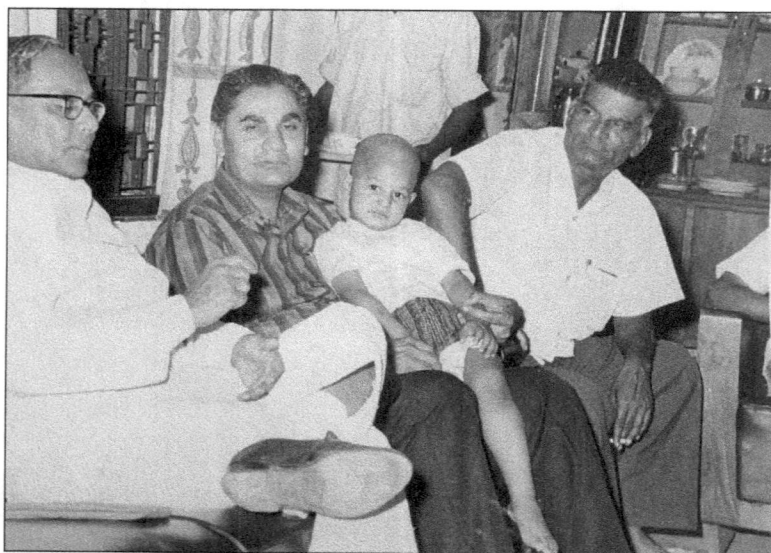

During Vivek's *mundan* ceremony in 1968:
K.C. Reddy, the then Governor of Madhya Pradesh, Balkrishan with
Vivek on his lap, and Kewal Krishan Uberoi

Lala Harbans Raj Uberoi

Lala Harbans Raj Uberoi's *kothi*,
situated at 27, Church Road, Ferozepur Cantonement

Mahesh Nivas, Rajeev's maternal grandparents' house,
at Dr Sadhuchand Road, Ferozepur

Rai Saheb Dr Sadhu Chand Vinayak,
Rajeev's maternal grandfather

Lala Amarnath Uberoi and his contribution to the Freedom Movement in India

Rajeev's great-grandfather, Lala Amarnath Uberoi

Rajeev's father, Balkrishan Uberoi in 1951

Rajeev's father, Balkrishan Uberoi in front of his *kothi*
at Sheikhupura, during his visit to Pakistan in 2003

UBEROI FAMILY FROM Gujranwala in Pakistan

Babu ji's father Lala Amarnath Uberoi was President of Indian National Congress in Sheikhupura, Punjab. A fearless man who built the most imposing home in the town. This picture is displayed at The Teen Murti Museum in New Delhi.

A rare photograph of Swami Shraddhanand, chairman, reception committee, with delegates to the Amritsar Congress, 1919. The Swami is seated fifth from left, flank ed by Pandit Motilal Nehru, who presided over the historic session, and Annie Besant. Jawaharlal Nehru is at the extreme left (ground row), Pandit Sundan Mohan Malaviya is sitting on the left of Mrs Besant.

Lala Amarnath Uberoi with Lokmanya Bal Gangadhar Tilak, Motilal Nehru, Swami Shraddhanand and Dr Annie Beasent at the Amritsar Congress, 1919. Jawaharlal Nehru is seen sitting on the ground in front of Lala Amarnath

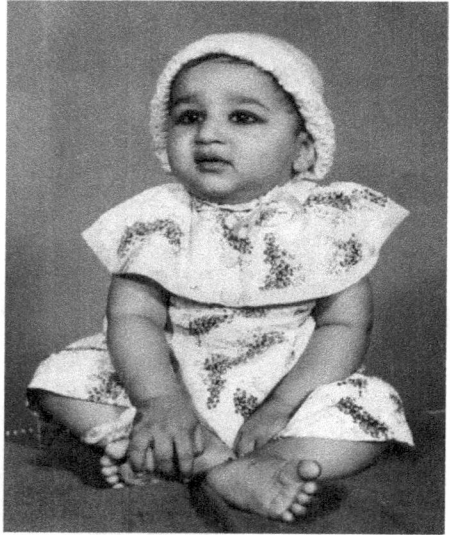

Rajeev as a baby!

Cousins: Aruna, Pradeep, Anil, Rajeev and Neelam, in 1957

Rajeev, as a tiny tot in 1960, trying to read an Algebra book
whilst holding it upside down!

Rajeev's birthday celebration, 1961

Vivek's mundan ceremony, 1968

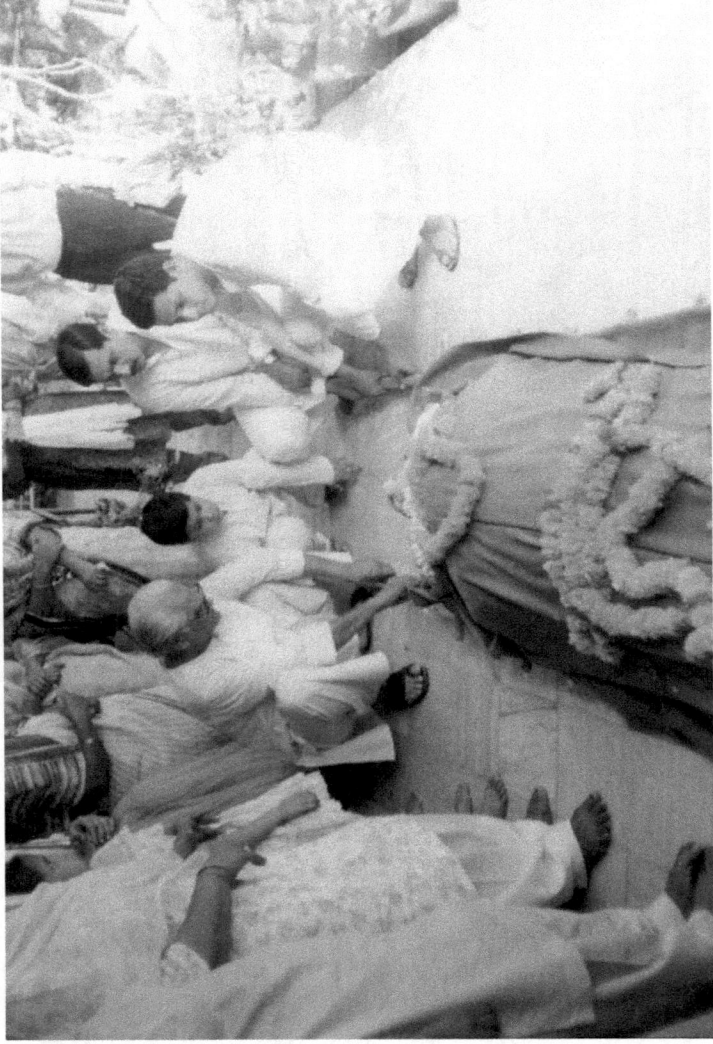

Last rites of our grandfather, Lala Harbans Raj Uberoi, in 1993.
Sitting: Balkrishan Uberoi, Kanav Rishi, Rajeev and Vivek

Ramesh Vinayak, Vinod Nanda,
Balkrishan Uberoi and Jitender Puri, 1966

Justice Loomba and Adarsha

to Sheikhupura with his family, it was one of the fastest growing towns in Punjab.

Harbansraj's decision to move to Sheikhupura with bag and baggage was a purely logistical decision. With Sheikhupura being made into a new district headquarter and the cases being split between the district court in Gujranwala and the new one being set up in Sheikhupura, Harbans Raj found himself travelling very frequently between the two towns. Though the distance between Gujranwala and Sheikhupura was only 45-50 kilometres, because the route did not fall on the Grand Truck Road, the modes of transportation available between the two towns were severely limited and the commute itself was very time consuming. In spite of this, for almost two years, Harbans Raj continued to maintain Gujranwala as his professional and personal base.

However, as his reputation in the legal circles in both Gujranwala and Sheikhupura grew stronger and his practise began doing well, it became apparent that things needed to change. He had junior lawyers and his father Lala Amarnath to guide him, but the volume of cases in Sheikhupura fast outnumbered those in Gujranwala. Being a newly established court, there were lesser number of skilled and well-established lawyers operating out of Sheikhupura, which meant that it was a young and open market for Harbans Raj to tap into. Aside from all this, there was also the fact that all the travelling to and fro between Gujranwala and Sheikhupura was beginning to take a toll on his health. Finally, in early 1924, Harbans Raj decided to move to Sheikhupura himself to set up his chamber there.

The Gujranwala set up, meanwhile, continued under the able guidance of Lala Amarnath and the team.

Accompanied by a trusted servant, Harbans Raj rented a house in Sheikhupura and quickly established a good legal practice in the town. He started appearing in the Lahore High Court regularly during the week and would return to Gujranwala on the weekends to spend time with the family. This routine continued for more than a year.

For the Uberoi family, these were years of stability and peace. Things had settled into a comfortable pattern. All of Harbansraj's siblings were on their way to becoming settled. The youngest of his brothers, about ten to twelve years his junior, had completed his education from Lahore. He was a very soft spoken boy with an elegant countenance and he looked up to Harbans Raj as a father figure, having been brought up by him after Lala Amarnath's arrest in 1919. In looks and build, he was quite similar to Harbansraj, and just like him, he was fond of a Western lifestyle too. Right after his graduation, he got an opportunity to work with a multinational company based in Singapore, and with the blessings of his elder brother, he left to embark on a new chapter in his life. He was, it appears, the first person in the family to go overseas for work.

Harbansraj's second brother was working in Lahore, as was his wife Sushila Devi's brother, who was a police inspector posted at the Anarkali Police Station in the city. His third sister, Saraswati, had also moved to Sheikhupura with her family as her husband practiced in the town's district court.

Harbansraj's own family was also growing. His wife, addressed by all his siblings as *Bhabhi*, was the anchor of the family even though she herself has barely twenty years old. Their first child, Kewal Krishan, was born in 1922, and they were blessed with a second son, whom they named Karta Krishan, in 1924. With her husband so caught up with work and living in a different town, Sushila Devi had her hands full with two young boys to look after and an entire household to manage. Lala Amarnath's imprisonment, the deaths of first his eldest daughter and then his second son-in-law were tragedies that had battered the family. But they all stayed united in the face of these troubles, and with the power of the family's full support behind them, Harbans Raj and Sushila Devi were not only able to bring up their children with great care, but were also able to steer the whole family back towards normalcy.

Amidst all of this, Harbans Raj acquired a large plot of land in what the Sheikhupura administration was calling Civil Lines, a new and developing colony that was located near the district court and the deputy commissioner's office. Sheikhupura's wealthy people, including lawyers and business, were being actively encouraged by the administration to buy land in this new colony and build houses there as part of its urbanisation drive. Even as he continued living and working out of rented premises, Harbans Raj started the construction of a kothi in Civil Lines which could eventually serve as the family home.

This house was a coming together of Harbansraj's grand aspirations and his inclination towards a decidedly

Western way of living. It had a large living room, six large bedrooms, a verandah in the front, a big backyard, a porch, a driveway, and a huge garden. There were separate quarters for servants on the property itself, and on an adjoining plot of land was a small orchard and a place to keep cattle for the family's dairy needs. The bungalow itself was made of red bricks and built in a contemporary style, with a high roof. There were fireplaces in all the rooms and there were two kitchens in the house, one where non-vegetarian Western food was cooked and the other were traditional vegetarian meals were cooked.

In 1925, a third son, Balkrishan, was born to Harbans Raj and Sushila Devi, and when he was just a few months old, the family moved to the newly constructed kothi in Sheikhupura. It was a welcome change for the family, especially for Harbansraj's two older boys as the house was modern, large, and had a lot of space for them to play in and their school was right across the road from their new home. The presence of his sister Saraswati in Sheikhupura was a big help in smoothening the process of transition for the family.

Over the next couple of years, Harbans Raj further cemented his roots in Sheikhupura. With a majority of his family now living in Sheikhupura and his father also spending more and more time in the town, Harbansraj's association with Gujranwala and Garjakh weakened and he spent all his energies on capitalising on the opportunities Sheikhupura presented to him for the expansion of his legal practise. Financially, the family was therefore very well off by now and was counted among the wealthy of

Sheikhupura. Harbansraj, now in his early forties, was taking forward the legacy of his father in both the social and political spheres by actively participating in the functioning of the Congress and the Arya Samaj, which got a great fillip here due to the expanding Khatri population. He was a leader in the truest sense, for not many can so drastically change the course of a family in one generation. He was single-handedly instrumental in bringing the family out of its misery when his father had been imprisoned and their world had turned topsy-turvy. He rose through his own shares of challenges and hardships, and guided the family back towards a better future. Had it not been for that fateful day in Gujranwala when the town's railway station was burnt down and damaged by an unruly mob, Lala Amarnath might have gone on to become a national leader, and his son, Harbans Raj would have had a very different career trajectory. But such are the destinies of families and individuals, that there is neither any controlling the paths they follow nor any predictions that can be made about their futures.

In the years that followed after the family moved into the new bungalow in Civil Lines, two daughters were born to Harbans Raj and Sushila Devi—Adarsha was born in 1931, followed by Swatantra in 1934. The name of the second daughter, Swatantra, was a reflection of the family's devotion to the cause of the national movement, since the word itself meant 'independent.' By this time, the late 1920s and the early 1930s that is, the Indian national movement had gained great momentum and the British administration had been forced to acknowledge the Indians' demand for greater political autonomy and authority. In the Lahore session of the Congress held in 1929, a resolution had been passed for *Purna Swaraj* or complete independence, which was a radical departure from the INC's earlier demand for home rule. Needless to say, the British government did not want such demands to get translated into public movements that could challenge its authority. It therefore came up with measures like the Government of India Act (1935) to try and appease Indian political aspirations without really having to dissolve its own hold over India.

This was also the time when internationally, Britain's global dominance was being threatened by Germany which was becoming economically and militarily stronger and was also expanding its sphere of influence under the leadership of Adolf Hitler. As tensions rose and friction increased, the world found itself getting swept into yet another conflict with the outbreak of the Second World War in 1939.

Between 1939 and 1945, when the war finally ended, there were many developments in the political arena in India. While the British tried to keep the situation under control, they had clearly underestimated the power of the Indian national movement. In 1942, when the Second World War was at its peak and Germany had captured practically the whole of Europe already, the Quit India Movement was launched in India under the leadership of Mahatma Gandhi, who had, by now, emerged as one of the most powerful and popular leaders of the national movement. Even as the British, left as they were with very limited options, scampered to save the situation, things began spiralling out of hand. They sent the Cripps Mission to India to discuss the possibility of a phased-out transfer of authority to democratically elected Indian representatives, with the idea of a full transfer of power to Indians as a prospective eventuality. But the Cripps Mission failed and went back to England with no tangible solution having being offered to diffuse the situation.

Further inflaming the political situation in India was Subhash Chandra Bose, who, with Japanese support, had formed the Indian National Army in Singapore and was attacking the British army from the east along with the Japanese army. By the time the war ended in the summer of 1945, even though Britain had emerged victorious, its economy was in complete shambles and its people were utterly battered. The global discourse on colonialism had also taken a negative term with colonial empires being severely criticised and the principle of democracy becoming the new mantra. With the situation weighing so heavily against them, the British prime minister, Sir Clement Attlee, was soon forced to announce that by June 1948, India would be given complete independence. To exhibit his commitment, he sent Lord Mountbatten to India in 1946 to execute a smooth transition of power.

However, it had become very clear by this point in time that India's independence from British rule would not simply be a matter of transferring power from the British Crown to elected Indian representatives. Because the British had long followed a policy of divide-and-rule while administering India since it suited their vested interests to do so, the situation on ground had become extremely communal with the Indian National Congress and the Muslim League, the two dominant political players, both advocating different visions of independent India. Where the INC was pushing for an independent undivided India, the Muslim League was asking for a separate independent state to be carved out on the basis of religious majority. The League's call for two separate nations found support in quite a few Muslim-majority regions across India, like Bengal in the east and Punjab in the west. The League also lobbied with the rulers of Muslim-dominated princely states like Hyderabad, Bhopal, Faridkot, Kasur, Junagarh, and Kashmir to back their demand for a separate country.

Sheikhupura was not oblivious to all this political turmoil. The death of Lala Lajpat Rai in 1928 due to injuries inflicted by the police during a lathi charge against a public demonstration, the arrests and secret hanging of revolutionaries like Bhagat Singh, Sukhdev, and Rajguru, were events that rocked the town. The town also responded enthusiastically to Mahatma Gandhi's calls for civil disobedience. Lala Harbans Raj took an active part in all the protest demonstrations that were held in Sheikhupura under the banner of the INC in these turbulent years. He had a lot of friends in the state level political circles and he quickly took charge of the District Congress committee, dedicating himself to building a strong district-level cadre for the Congress.

But even as calls for complete independence rang out loud and clear in every lane and alleyway in Sheikhupura, there were communal undercurrents everywhere. While Muslims outweighed the Hindus and the Sikhs in terms of population numbers, they were economically weaker as most of them worked as farmhands and menial workers while majority of the landownership, trade, commerce, and wealth rested with the Hindus and the Sikhs. In addition, most of the educated class, lawyers, doctors, and engineers were predominantly non-Muslims. Even in the senior echelons of the administration, it was the non-Muslims who dominated. Also, the presence of two important Sikh places of worship in Sheikhupura, the Shiver Deva Baba Nanak and the Nankana Sahib, made it a very significant place for the Sikhs. So strong was the Hindu and Sikh presence in Sheikhupura that as the prospect of India's partition became fait accompli and people began speculating about how the lines would be drawn and which areas would go to which country, most of them believed that both Lahore and Sheikhupura would remain in India. In fact, during the later part of 1946, many Hindus from the North West Frontier Province (NWFP) and nearby areas found it safer to move their families to Sheikhupura district.

With confusion and chaos rising and communal tensions simmering, the local administration of Sheikhupura formed a peace committee to extend comfort and confidence to both the communities and foster the growth of mutual trust. It held special meetings with the police and with social and political leaders to regularly discuss the situation and ensure that law and order were maintained in the district. Lala Harbans Raj played an active role in these peace-keeping efforts and regularly visited Muslim-dominated areas to make speeches that encouraged the people to stay united and not pay heed to communal rumours. While all of this did help in building harmony between the communities in the initial stages, the hasty manner in which the British handled the whole process of transferring power whipped up an unimaginable wave of communal frenzy in the days and months ahead.

When Lord Mountbatten arrived in India in 1946, the agreed upon date for the final handing over of power was June 1948, but in early 1947, Mountbatten decided to complete this mammoth process by August itself. With hardly any preparation about how the actual process would unfold administratively and on ground, he announced the formation of the Radcliffe Committee which would decide how the actual division of India on religious grounds would take place. Right after this announcement, in May 1947, Mr Radcliffe, a lawyer by profession, landed in India. This was his first time in the country. With barely any ideas about the social, cultural, political, and economic realities of India, Radcliffe went through the motions of collecting data and holding hearings to enable an informed decision being made, and on 14 August 1947, announced where the borders dividing India and the new state of Pakistan would run through. That things were done in a great tearing hurry was attested to by Kuldip Nayar, an eminent Indian journalist who had moved with his family from Pakistan to India during the Partition. Nayar met Radcliffe in 1971 and was told that the latter had almost decided to give Lahore to India but had instead clubbed it with Pakistan at the very last minute. This was the kind of arbitrary approach that led ultimately to the Partition becoming one of the bloodiest events in India's history.

Like most others, Lala Harbans Raj was certain that Sheikhupura was a safe haven for him and his family and that it would be a part of India. He had no reason to think about uprooting everyone from Sheikhupura and moving them elsewhere for the sake of safety. His children were all doing well. Kewal Krishan had taken up a job in Jabalpur after his graduation. Karta Krishan was working as a manager at the Bank of Lahore. Balkrishan had also graduated and was pursuing his law degree, well on his way to becoming a third-generation lawyer. Adarsha had taken admission in the Girls' College in Sheikhupura and the youngest, Swatantra, was in the final year of her schooling. Harbans Raj himself was more involved in his social and political commitments. His legal practise was thriving by now and he was a very well respected figure in the social, administrative, and political circles of Sheikhupura. When the wheels of his and his family's life were rolling so smoothly, why would he think of leaving it all behind and shifting to a new place and starting from scratch?

But the Muslim League, which was in power in Punjab, had different plans for the entire region: to put it simply, it wanted to retain Lahore and its surrounding areas, all wealthy towns and cities, as parts of Pakistan. While Muhammad Ali Jinnah, its leader, constantly claimed that they wanted a peaceful transfer of power, on ground, systematically and well ahead of the announcement of the Radcliffe award, the League was playing a different game by consolidating its base in the administrative and political machinery of the region. In January 1947 itself, it posted Muslim loyalists in key positions in the administrative, police, and revenue services with the clear mandate to protect the Muslim population of the region while encouraging, and at times even persecuting the Sikhs and the Hindus and forcing them to flee to India. It even brought in army contingents, like the Pukhtoon regiment, that had a strong religious affinity with its beliefs. The situation was further aggravated by a whole host of other factors and elements. There were, for instance, Muslim clerics who were raising religious fervour amongst the public by making inflammatory speeches that urged the people to rise up together in defence of their religion. Another dangerous development was the influx of Muslim fundamentalists from the tribal frontier provinces who cared not a whit for such things as communal harmony. These fundamentalists had the tacit backing of the Muslim League state government which was led by Sir Sikandar Hayat Khan, the chief minister of Punjab and a man heavily influenced by Jinnah, and while the local population itself maintained a largely tolerant attitude towards their Hindu and Sikh neighbours, the fundamentalists went around spreading their communal agenda. Ultimately, when the violence erupted, according to some estimates more than 10,000 people were killed in Sheikhupura itself within the first week and there is no record of just how many non-Muslim women were kidnapped, raped, and forced to convert to Islam for the sake of their survival. But it must be admitted here that the senseless killings and the violence ran on both sides of the line that Radcliffe so hurriedly drew across the Indian landmass on 13 August 1947. In fact, one of the last straws that completely undid all efforts at maintaining peace and order were the horrifying stories of violence against their community that Muslims coming from East Punjab, Bihar, and the United Provinces brought with them. These stories of people being killed, shops and homes being looted, and women being raped and abducted severed the last restrains of sanity and humanity.

Radcliffe made the ill-fated announcement about the partitioning of India on the radio at 2 a.m. in the morning on 13 August. The next day, on 14 August, Pakistan was declared an independent state, and a few days later, around 17 or 18 August, it finally became clear that Sheikhupura and Lahore were going to be parts of Pakistan. Chaos and mayhem swept through the region. The district administration now openly supported mobs that went around hunting down non-Muslim residents of Sheikhupura. There was looting, arson, merciless killing, and the rest, as they say, was history, albeit a gruesome and ugly history.

In the Uberoi household, the entire family, all except Kewal Krishan who was in Jabalpur, were together at Sheikhupura. Lala Harbans Raj was busy with his peace committee commitments, and even though there was an element of fear in everyone's hearts, they were somewhat confident that adequate protection would be provided to the Hindus and the Sikhs by the local administration and the army which was, at this point in time, neutral in allegiance. The possibility of having to forcibly leave everything behind was not something that had sunk in yet. However, some close Muslim friends of the family did warn Lala Harbans Raj about the existence of lists prepared by Muslim fanatics containing names of people who had to be eliminated, with the nights of 17 and 18 August being tentative dates of the attacks. It seemed that Lala Harbans Raj and his family's names featured prominently on these lists.

The morning of 18 August was tense but seemingly normal. Lala Harbans Raj got ready and left home for his regular peace committee meetings. His wife and the children were all at home and as a precaution, the family's clothes, valuables, and money were kept packed. At around 5 p.m., while Lala Harbans Raj was still out, his sister Saraswati, accompanied by a trusted servant, came to the Uberoi house and asked Sushila Devi and the four children to quickly shift to her own house. She was close to the wife of a well-placed Muslim police inspector, and she had gotten information that some miscreants planned to attack the Uberoi kothi the same night and that they would not hesitate to slaughter its residents. Without wasting any time, Sushila Devi and the children quickly left their kothi and moved to Saraswati Devi's house, but there was no way of informing Lala Harbans Raj about this development without loosing precious time.

A little later in the evening, at around 6:30 p.m., when he was returning home in his horse driven carriage, Lala Harbans Raj spotted a huge column of fire rising up into the sky from the direction of the family house. A Muslim mob had broken into the house, looted and ransacked everything inside, and then, not finding anyone inside, they had put the whole house on fire. To say that panic and dread must have held Lala Harbansraj's heart in a vice-like grip would be an understatement. Thankfully though, as

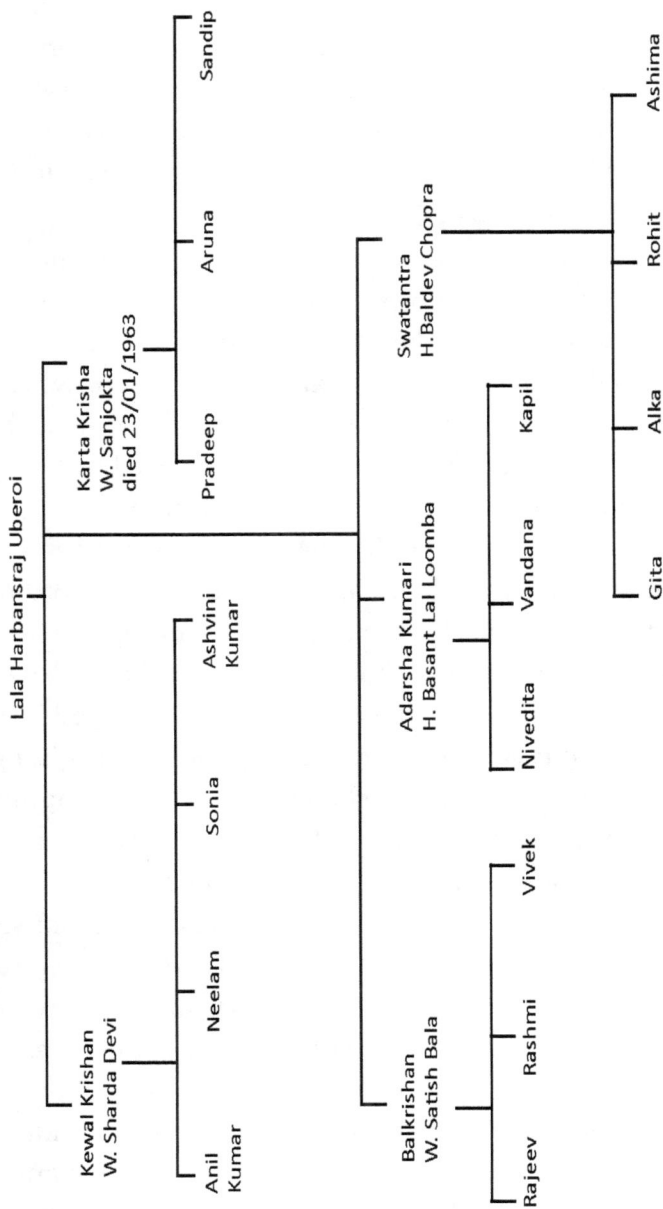

Lala Harbansraj Uberoi

Kewal Krishan
W. Sharda Devi

Anil Kumar · Neelam · Sonia · Ashvini Kumar

Karta Krisha
W. Sanjokta
died 23/01/1963

Pradeep · Aruna · Sandip

Balkrishan
W. Satish Bala

Rajeev · Rashmi · Vivek

Adarsha Kumari
H. Basant Lal Loomba

Nivedita · Vandana · Kapil

Swatantra
H. Baldev Chopra

Gita · Alka · Rohit · Ashima

27/01/1969

he sped towards the burning kothi, he spotted one of their trusted Muslim servants waiting right beside the road a little distance from the house. The man quickly informed him that the whole family had fled to Saraswati Devi's house and that they were all safe there. Without wasting a second, Lala Harbans Raj raced to his sister's house to be reunited with his family.

Later that evening, when it was dark and quiet outside, Balkrishan, against everyone's wishes, went back to the Uberoi house to collect whatever valuables he could find in the smouldering ruins. But while he was there with a Muslim servant in tow, people got wind of his presence and an angry mob quickly collected outside the house. As they charged into the house and began hunting for him, Balkrishan had barely enough time to climb up the 8 feet high wall in the backyard and jump into the compound of the Muslim family that lived next door. Although fearful for their own safety, the Muslim family allowed Balkrishan to stay the night, but early next morning, they urged him to leave, lest the miscreants ransack their house for giving refuge to a non-Muslim. Balkrishan had two options at this point—he could either try and get to one of the two refugee camps which had just been opened up and were being managed by the army, or he could go to his aunt's house, see if his family was still there, and then decide on the next move. Outside, the morning sun was rising and there were groups of hoodlums already out patrolling the streets, hungry for any victim that they could lay their hands on. Could he really reach his aunt's house without running into the mobs and leading them right to where his family was? Clearly, it would be much wiser and safer for him to try and reach one of the refugee camps. The family that had sheltered him through the night once again came to his rescue. They dressed him up like a common Muslim man and led him outside, hoping he would reach the refugee camp without encountering any danger on the way.

Meanwhile, the rest of the Uberoi family had spent a night filled with great anxiety and fear because Balkrishan had not come back home. With the situation outside worsening with every passing hour, they couldn't venture out to look for him either. Sheikhupura was clearly no longer a safe place for any of them.

By morning, the situation became graver still as people had come to know that Lala Harbans Raj and his entire family were hiding in his sister's bungalow. But Saraswati Devi's friend, the wife of the police inspector, heard that trouble was afoot and she quickly had the whole family brought over to her own house before an agitated and armed mob could reached the Mahna's residence. The girls and the women were hidden inside the police inspector's house, and because Muslim women practice purdha, the Uberoi women were all able to stay safe. Lala Harbansraj, now dressed like a Muslim farmhand, was hidden in the room where straw for milk cattle was stored. The crowd, meanwhile, had reached the inspector's bungalow, having heard about the close association between the former's wife and Saraswati Devi. When they insisted on searching the house, the police inspector could not refuse without making them think that he had something to hide! However, he told the crowd that no one could damage any part of the house and that the women in his family practised purdah and wouldn't, under any circumstances, reveal their faces to the men. The crowd agreed to these conditions, and after searching for the Uberoi family but not finding anyone who looked either like an Uberoi or a Hindu, they eventually left the bungalow.

Still dressed in Muslim attire, the Uberoi family was hurriedly bundled into police vehicles as soon as it was deemed safe enough for them to come out of their hiding places. They were then taken to the refugee camp, which was the safest place for them at that point in time, secured as it was by an army contingent. This was, unfortunately, not the same refugee camp that Balkrishan had made his way to earlier in the morning.

The family spent the next three days at the refugee camp living through what can only be described as a nightmare. There was still no news of Balkrishan. No one had any idea whether he was safe and alive or if the mobs had gotten to him. And there was simply no way of finding anything out. Things were not easy within the camp either. Small tents had been allocated to the family and some food had been provided too, but there were no provisions for toilets. During the night, from within the camp, they could hearing angry mobs shouting "Allah U Akbar" outside as they went about looting and destroying Sikh and Hindu premises and killing innocent people. The night sky was lit up with tall fires from all the homes and shops that the mobs were setting fire to. All around, there was only panic. There was no source of any authentic information, no radios that could provide regular, even if selective updates about the situation outside. The rumour mills were working overtime, and every new entrant to the refugee camp brought with them gory tales of the violence that had erupted all over Sheikhupura. The news that trains full of dead bodies of slaughtered Muslims from Amritsar were arriving in Lahore acted as the last nail in the coffin, and so severe was the backlash across Pakistan Punjab that the army had to be called in for the safe evacuation of the Sikhs and Hindus sheltering in the refugee camps.

Finally, around 23 August, an army column comprising of British and Sikh soldiers arrived from Lahore and replaced the Baluch Regiment that had been guarding the refugee camps until then. All the refugees were put inside army trucks, and accompanied by armed guards, they were moved from Sheikhupura to Amritsar. It took more than 18 hours for the first convoy to reach Amritsar, which was on the Indian side of the newly drawn border. The convoy travelled via Lahore and Attari, and the entire route was littered with the decaying corpses of those who had attempted the same journey, but because they were unarmed and unaccompanied by an army convoy, they had fallen victim to bloodthirsty mobs. The air was heavy with the stench of blood and death. The whole situation was inhuman and exhibited what religious fanaticism and greed could do.

By the time the convoy reached Amritsar, it was dark, and after getting themselves registered with the camp authorities, the Uberois were allotted tents to live in. But there was nothing to sleep on, no clothes they could change into, no money to buy the basic things they needed. They were given some food, but even that was served directly into their hands as there were no plates and bowls available for the hundreds and thousands of refugees who had started pouring into the camps. The administration was absolutely unprepared for dealing with the exploding situation, but then again, no one could have predicted that the partition of India would become one of the biggest instances of forced migrations in the history of the subcontinent.

For the moment though, Lala Harbansraj, Sushila Devi, Karta Krishan, Adarsha, and Swatantra had reached Amritsar, and they were all safe and together. But there was still no information about Balkrishan.

Chapter 5

AMRITSAR – DELHI

❈

Everyday, there were announcements that were made in the refugee camp in Amritsar about the names and the villages of new arrivals in the camp so that people could find their missing kith and kin. The Uberois were not the only ones with a family member missing. Almost every person, every family in the refugee camp had one or more people who had gone missing in the violent chaos that marked the Partition. With every passing day, the Uberois found their hope growing weaker as they continued to pray for some news of Balkrishan. It was on their third day in the camp that they heard Balkrishan's name being announced on the camp's rudimentary public announcement system. The family was jubilant and they rushed to be reunited with him.

When Balkrishan later recounted his journey to Amritsar, it became evident that it had been fraught with danger. After having escaped the angry mob that had attacked the Uberoi kothi while he was still inside it, he had taken on a fake name, dressed himself as a common Muslim man, and cautiously made his way to one of the refugee camps in Sheikhupura. But he had been unable to actually reach the Rice Mill refugee camp that was guarded by the Punjab Regiment and had to instead hide in a truck that was carrying straw. He had also darkened his face in order to avoid being recognised by anyone as Lala Harbansraj's son. He had reached Amritsar a couple of days after the rest of the family because it had taken him time to find a place for himself in a convoy. But there he finally was, happy and relieved that all of them had survived the holocaust and were together again.

The refugee camp at Amritsar was perhaps the largest in the region and thousands of refugees poured into this safe sanctuary from all across Pakistan. Being a border town that was just about 40 kilometres from Lahore, Amritsar was the entry point into India for refugees from West Pakistan. In fact, so great was the inflow of refugees that many of them had to be shifted to other camps in cities like New Delhi, Ambala, Haridwar, and Dehradun.

It is interesting to note that even though Amritsar was the second largest town after Lahore in undivided Punjab and was a Muslim dominated district, it was kept in India since Harmandir Sahib, the holiest shrine of the Sikhs was in Amritsar.

The camp in Amritsar was largely a makeshift camp that was spread over a large open area outside the city.

There were no buildings whatsoever in the camp, and even the administrative office was actually nothing but a large tent with a few tables and chairs that served as a rudimentary reception area where the registration of refugees was done. It also housed a lost-and-found table. The rest of the camp premises were taken over by tents that had been pitched in rows upon rows and were allotted to families with women and children. The others were asked to fend for themselves.

When the army vehicles carrying refugees arrived at the camp, the camp authorities first recorded the details of the refugees. Their name, age, where they were coming from, names of the family members travelling with them, all these details were noted down. They were then given a number, which was, for all practical purposes, their new identity. Once done with this registration process, they were allotted a place in the camp and given some food packets. But beyond that, life in the refugee camp was very challenging and depressing. One had to stand in line for everything, for food, for bathing, for washing, for making enquiries about missing family members. Everything was scarce—food, clothes, water, tents. This was not surprising because so great was the deluge of refugees coming into India that the infrastructure of the refugee camps, already stretched thin, was almost at a breaking point. There was nothing a person living in one of these camps could do other than have hope and wait for something to happen or meet someone who could be a beacon of light and help them rebuild their lives outside the camps.

The time that the Uberois spent in the refugee camp was the lowest point in the family's history. After the reunion with Balkrishan, they took a handful of days to settle down in the camp the best they could. They went around the camp looking for anyone familiar, and followed the daily announcements about the new entrants to the camp with great attention. Lala Harbans Raj tried to connect with his friends who were already in India, but there was so much of chaos both inside and outside the camp that it was impossible to connect with anyone.

In the third week of their stay in the camp, lady luck finally smiled on the Uberois when they heard an announcement being made for the Uberoi family from Sheikhupura to come to the camp's administrative office. Lala Harbans Raj rushed to the administrative office and found Gopal Handa, the son of his wife's nephew, Pran Nath Handa, waiting for him there. The Handas, as it turned out, had been looking for the Uberoi family for a while, and now that they had been finally found, it was time to move out from the refugee camp to the house of Pran Nath Handa.

The Uberois stayed with Pran Nath Handa, an inspector posted in Amritsar, for more than six months. They were among the lucky ones, for not only had they been able to leave the camp within a very short period of time, but Lala Harbans Raj was also able to finally connect with his friends who helped him in getting a respectable job as a regional manager with Sunlite Insurance, a Lahore-based insurance company that had moved its operations to Delhi after the partition of India. He moved to Delhi, leaving the family with the Handas for a couple of months until they could figure out what was to be done. The eldest of Lala Harbansraj's sons, Kewal Krishan was safe in

Jabalpur, where he was working. Karta Krishan had lost his job because the Bank of Lahore, where he had worked prior to fleeing to India, had no operations in India. But he managed to turn things around for himself when he landed a job with the Ministry of Rehabilitation which had been created for the rehabilitation and settlement of refugees from Pakistan. This job, however, took him away from the family since he got posted in Kolkata. Balkrishan, who had not yet completed his law degree, took admission in the Government Law College at Simla, and the girls, Adarsha and Swatantra, stayed at home as most schools and colleges had not started their academic session for the year on account of the Partition.

Once Lala Harbans Raj was settled in Delhi, he moved Sushila Devi and the girls to Delhi to be with him. Sushila Devi's youngest brother, Dwarkanath Handa, was also working in Delhi. He was posted in the Vice Regal Lodge and was allotted a house in the Delhi Cantonment where the four Uberois joined him. The girls found it very difficult to live in Delhi as they were not use to the ways of living in a big sprawling city. Swatantra, the youngest, was admitted in a girls' school in Lodhi Estate and she had to commute back and forth by public transport, something she had never seen or done in Sheikhupura. As the story goes, one day she got lost while coming home from school and there was complete panic and pandemonium in family. The ordeal only ended when she managed to reach home safe and sound very late in the evening.

Within a few months of moving to Delhi, the family found itself at the crossroads once again when Lala Harbans Raj was transferred to Agra, a totally new place where they knew absolutely no one. Lala Harbans Raj was not sure if it would be a wise decision to move the family all over again as the girls had now resumed their studies and they needed to have some continuity and stability in their lives. Also, the safety and security of the three women was a big concern for Harbans Raj since all the boys were scattered all across the country — Kewal Krishan was in Jabalpur, Karta Krishan was in Kolkata, and Balkrishan was in Simla — and he himself was entirely tied up with his new job.

Even when it came to the extended family, Harbansraj's siblings were living in different cities spread across North India. His brother Harsukhraj who had been working in the Punjab National Bank (PNB) in Lahore, was now posted in the PNB branch in Amritsar. The second brother Hardhanraj was in Dhariwal, where his in-laws had settled, and the youngest brother, Harpratap was working in Lucknow. Of his sisters, Balwant was living with her married daughter; Saraswati Devi had relocated from Sheikhupura to Palwal with her family, and the youngest sister, Leelawati Kakar, was settled in Ferozepur.

After a lot of deliberation and discussion, Lala Harbans Raj finally decided to move the family to Ferozepur. This would be the third time in two years that they would be uprooting themselves to move to a new place and set up a family home, but given the circumstances, it was a small price to pay for having the whole family safe and alive.

Chapter 6

FEROZEPUR

T he town of Ferozepur draws its name from its founder, Firoz Shah Tughlak. Established in the 14th century near the river Sutlej, one of the five main rivers of Punjab, Ferozepur has a semi arid climate with fertile alluvial soil irrigated by a network of canals. The town fell under British rule in around 1835 and was subsequently made the base from where the Anglo-Sikh Wars were fought in 1845-46 and 1848-49, post which the Khalsa empire was annexed by the British.

As a British cantonment town, Ferozepur developed steadily. It had a large agricultural produce market along with numerous cotton ginning factories and weaving units. It was well connected to both Delhi and Lahore by rail and had a bustling trading centre. There were schools and colleges for both boys and girls. The town's infrastructural setup was good as was the law and order situation, and it was known as a relatively safe district. The more urban parts of Ferozepur were predominantly Sikh and Hindu, while in the rural areas the population ratio was split almost equally between the Hindus and the Muslims. There is an interesting anecdote about how Ferozepur, in spite of its significant Muslim population and its position adjoining Pakistan, was given to India under the Radcliffe award. Until about 6 August 1947, Ferozepur and Gurdaspur were included in what was to be the new nation of Pakistan. The boundary maps and documents from the office of Radcliffe indicate that this decision to give Ferozepur and Gurdaspur to Pakistan was subject to agreement amongst the members of the boundary commission and the approval of Lord Mountbatten. However, in the end, both were given to India.

Post the partition of India, Ferozepur's fate changed dramatically. It was actually shocking to see how the fortunes of the city declined as it became a border town. Most of the town's Muslim population migrated to Pakistan and it saw a steep fall in economic activity. The two wars with Pakistan in 1965 and 1971 were the last nail in its coffin and it crumbled under neglect and a fast shrivelling economy.

But all of this aside, back in 1948, what really influenced Lala Harbansraj's decision to shift his family to Ferozepur was the fact that his youngest sister Leelawati was settled there as the wife of one of the town's well established landlords. Leelawati and her family's presence in Ferozepur would afford Lala Harbans Raj and his family a degree of comfort and security that was invaluable.

Once the decision was taken, Lala Harbans Raj quickly put things in motion. A large house was rented and the family moved to Ferozepur by early 1949. The girls quickly resumed their education, and for the next few years, the entire focus of the family was on setting up their lives once again. The house the family had rented was opened to all their relatives who had lived through situations similar to their own during the Partition, and people poured in, looking for the familial support and comfort that the Uberois were offering.

Gradually, things began improving for the family. Lala Harbansraj's regular income from the insurance company was adequate to meet the household's expenses and the family was able to maintain a decent standard of living. Harbans Raj had also filed a claim for compensation with the Ministry of Rehabilitation which allowed refugees who had left behind their properties in Pakistan to seek financial compensation for their loss. Once a claim was evaluated, its authenticity verified through ownership documents, and its value appraised, the claimant was eligible to buy properties taken over by the government since their original Muslim owners had left India during the Partition. The whole process was quite cumbersome and time consuming, but by 1951, Lala Harbansraj's claims were settled and he became eligible to bid for properties listed by the Ministry of Rehabilitation. This was again a time-consuming process, more so as Harbans Raj was working in Agra and the claims could only be made in and around Ferozepur, where the family was. Finally, Harbans Raj was able to acquire a large bungalow in the cantonment area in Ferozepur. It was a majestic bungalow spread over 1.27 acres of land, and built by the Nawab of Mamdat, a principality in Punjab. It had eight bedrooms, a verandah, two large drawing rooms, a large courtyard, a long drive in, a porch, a sprawling garden which included a fruit orchard with a well, and a number of servants' quarters. Additionally, Harbans Raj also acquired four shops opposite the Ferozepur bus stand and around 50 acres of land in Faridkot and Rampur in the United Provinces. The bungalow and the shops were rented out, which supplemented the family's source of income and ensured that Lala Harbans Raj never became dependent on any of his children for any financial assistance ever. The agricultural land, however, was difficult to manage and was eventually sold off.

Meanwhile, the family itself was growing as the children got married one after the other. The two elder sons, Kewal Krishan and Karta Krishan had gotten engaged in 1946 while the family was still in Sheikhupura. But because of the havoc that the Partition had wreaked on everyone's lives, their marriages had been delayed. Thankfully though, the families of their respective fiancées had survived the Partition violence and had managed to settle in India. The first to now get married was Kewal Krishan, who was engaged to Sharda Chopra, the daughter of a PCS officer posted in Simla. They were married in 1949, and over the years the couple was blessed with five children — Anil, Neelam, Nalini, Sonia, and Ashwin. Kewal Krishan's work would eventually make him and his family move to Khandwa, where he would go on to become a leading forest contractor. Our families, however, remained close. We would meet them during our summer holidays annually, and as Khandwa was close to Bhopal, there were frequent visits in between as well. Also, Kewal Krishan's two elder children, Ankil and Neelam, did their graduation from Bhopal, which was where we—my parents and my siblings—stayed.

The next in line was Karta Krishan, who was engaged to Sanjokta Sehgal, the daughter of Dr Baldev Raj Sehgal. The Uberois and the Sehgals had been neighbours in Sheikhupura before the Partition, and the latter had settled in Delhi after leaving Sheikhupura. Karta Krishan and Sanjokta's marriage was solemnised in Ferozepur. After working in the Ministry of Rehabilitation for a couple of years, Karta Krishan resumed working for the Punjab National Bank when he got married. He was posted in various cities across India, like Lucknow, Bhopal, and Mokama to name a few. Karta Krishan and Sanjokta were blessed with three children—Aruna, Pradeep, and Sandip (whose name was later changed to Vivek). Unfortunately, due to a severe brain stroke, Karta Krishan died in 1963 and for sometime after his death, Sanjokta moved to Ferozepur to be with the rest of the family. Later, when she got a job with Punjab National Bank, she shifted to Delhi along with her children.

In 1953, Balkrishan was married to Satish Vinayak, whose father, Dr Sadhu Chand Vinayak, was one of the leading doctors of Ferozepur and a very well respected person. About the particular life paths that Balkrishan and

Satish, my parents, took, there will be much later.

Adarsha, the elder of Lala Harbans Raj and Sushila Devi's two daughters, was sixteen years of age when the Partition happened. As the family settled in Ferozepur and made a tentative but determined return towards normalcy, she pursued her studies and completed both her graduation and post graduation from Ferozepur itself, after which a good match was found for her, and in 1953, she was married to Basant Lal Loomba. Basant Lal was a lawyer by education. He joined the judicial services of the United Provinces and was eventually appointed as the justice of the Allahabad High Court, from the Lucknow Bench. Adarsha worked as well, and became an acclaimed teacher. She went on to become the principal of a school in Lucknow. The couple was blessed with three children—Nivedita, Vandana, and Kapil. The family settled in Lucknow while both the daughters eventually settled in New Delhi.

Swatantra, the youngest of the siblings, was barely ten years old on the eve of the Partition. Just like her elder sister, she too completed her education in Ferozepur and was married in 1957 to Baldev Raj Chopra, an engineer who worked in the Irrigation Department of the Punjab government. They had four children—Geeta, Alka, Rohit, and Ashima. The family stayed in Ferozepur till 1972, when they moved away for work.

Once all their children were married, Lala Harbans Raj and Sushila Devi shifted from the large rented bungalow to a smaller bungalow named The Rose, on the Mall Road. The bungalow stood right opposite the Company Garden where my grandfather regularly went for his morning and

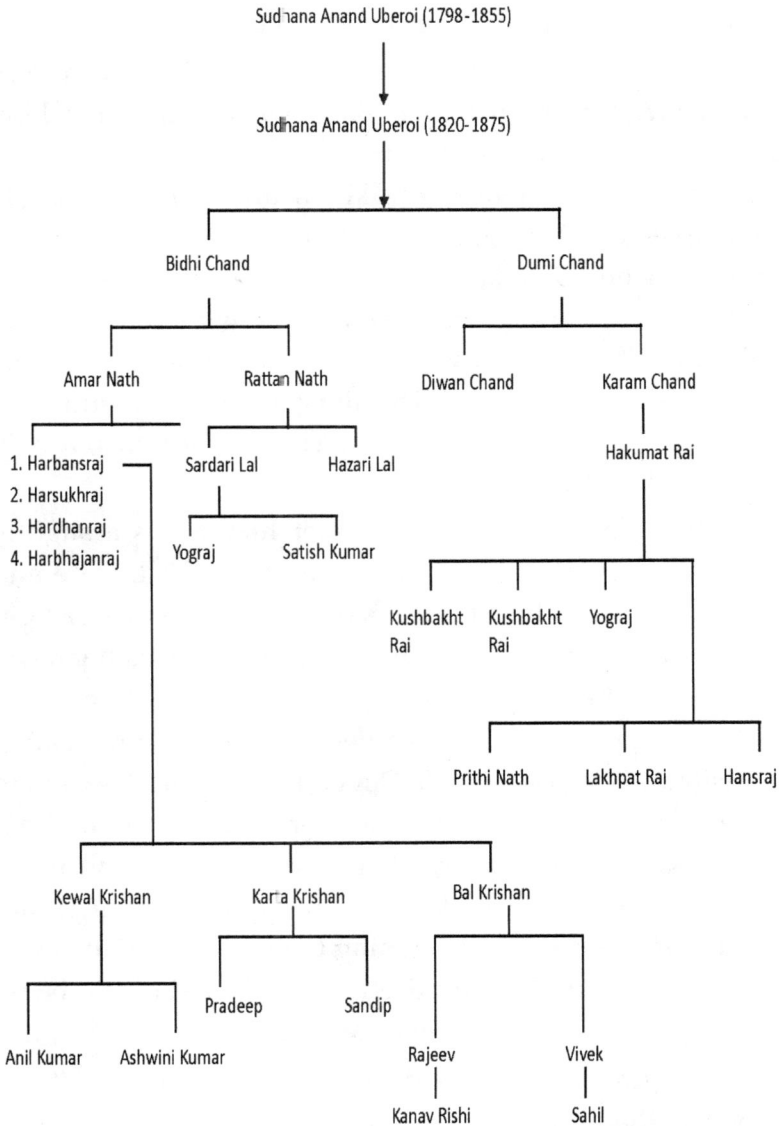

evening walks. The Rose was a red brick colonial bungalow with a high roof, verandahs both in the front and the back, a courtyard, and a small kitchen garden.

Both Lala Harbans Raj and Sushila Devi led a very frugal life. My grandfather, Bauji as we all called him, had a towering personality. He was six feet tall, fair, lean, and thin, and he wore only khadi after having actively participated in the Quit India Movement in 1942. Every time he went out, he would be dressed in a perfectly starched kurta and pyjama, and in the winters, he would wear his black achkan which added even more charisma to his erect figure. He carried himself very well, and even when he started using a walking stick for support, it only added to his elegance.

My grandmother, on the other hand, was a slightly built five feet tall woman who was very affectionate and loving. She was almost always dressed in a white or light blue salwar kameez with a large dupatta covering her head. She did all the cooking in the house, although there was one part-time servant who came in every day for washing utensils and clothes. Sushila Devi rarely went out, except to Arya Samaj gatherings, and she spent a fair amount of her time talking to the birds she fed every day in the mornings and the evenings. Years later, when my father bought her a transistor, she enjoyed listening to music on it. However, Bauji reprimanded her for listening to the radio, and being a very meek person, she never retorted back.

My grandparents had very limited conversations between them. Their roles in the household were very strictly laid out. While Bauji took care of all the financial and worldly matters, my grandmother was responsible for running the household. She never had any money of her own and it seems to me that she did not even need it as she rarely went out.

At times, I remember wondering how two people with such contrasting personalities could have gotten married. What had made Bauji decide to get married to my grandmother? Rather childishly, I had once put this question to my grandmother, and in response, she had laughed till her eyes had started watering. She told me that it had been days after her marriage that she had had her first glimpse of Bauji. There were stories about Bauji being very upset with the match, but with time, things settled down and my grandparents enjoyed more than 50 years of married life together!

In retrospect, I realise that my grandmother was a very noble soul. She had no financial demands and was happy in whatever situation she found herself in. She never ever spoke ill of anyone or anything and had no expectations from anyone, and instead she made sacrifices for the family her whole life. To me, she was an ideal grandmother, pampering me with hot parathas slathered with white butter that I simply loved to eat while sitting on the kitchen floor with her. She played a silent but extremely pivotal role in building up the family for generations to come.

My paternal grandparents lived in Ferozepur till about 1972, when they finally moved to Bhopal to stay with Balkrishan and his family due to my grandmother's failing health. Lala Harbans Raj had continued to work with Sunlite Insurance till he reached his superannuation in 1956 and in the years following his retirement, he had led a slow and quiet life, preferring to spend his time reading books and participating in the activities of the Arya Samaj. Before they left for Bhopal, my grandfather disposed off his properties, except for the bungalow which he passed on to my father, Balkrishan. Until the very end, my grandparents lived life on their own terms and never relied on their children for financial support.

My association with Ferozepur was made doubly stronger by the fact that even my maternal grandparents were based in the same town. Rai Sahib Dr Sadhu Chand Vinayak, my mother's father, was, as mentioned before, a leading general practitioner in Ferozepur and was very well respected in the whole region. In spite of having a flourishing medical practice, he was very actively engaged in many social and educational activities. During the British period, he was awarded the title of Rai Sahib, equivalent to the title of 'sir' in England, for his contributions to the fields of medicine, social work, and education.

As a student, Sadhu Chand was very bright and had been awarded a scholarship to attend the Lahore Medical College. After completing his studies in medicine, he served in the medical corps of the British Indian Army before settling in Ferozepur and establishing his medical practice there. Being the eldest in the family, he took upon himself the task of settling his five siblings — three sisters and two brothers. He was a very soft spoken person and a gentleman of the highest order. He headed the Red Cross Society, was the president of the Blind Home Trust, was active in the DAV College Trust, and even established a public library in the memory of his father in Ferozepur. He was married to Sita Devi, the daughter of Prof. Chopra, who retired as the principal of Maharaja College in Patiala and settled in Lahore post retirement. Sita Devi was a staunch nationalist and Arya Samaji. Together, they had five children, one son and four daughters. They were a very well-knit family and Sita Devi, in a stark contrast to how parent-children relationships functioned in those times, was a friend, philosopher, and guide not only to her children, but to her seven grandchildren as well.

Saroj was the eldest child in the Vinayak household and was married to Ganesh Lal Sondhi in 1951. Ganesh Lal was a lawyer employed by the government of India and was posted in Bombay. The couple had two sons — Rakesh and Rajesh, and they have now settled in the United States.

My mother, Satish, was the second daughter, and after her marriage to my father, the couple moved to Bhopal. Sashi, the third daughter, was married to Dr Vinod Chander Nanda, a professor in mathematics at the Bhabha Atomic Research Centre in Bombay in 1957. They were also blessed with two sons, Sanjiv and Vipul, and are now settled in Chandigarh.

My grandparents' only son, Ramesh Chand Vinayak, had his initial education from Lawrence School, Sanawar, and then went on to acquire a degree in metallurgy engineering from the Birla Institute of Technology, Ranchi. Post that, he went to the Michigan Institute of Technology, Chicago for his post graduation. He was married to Veena Bahl in 1966. Ramesh Chand's wedding was a very elaborate affair. The barat went from Ferozepur to Jalandhar in a bus since that was where the wedding was to be held. For me, the highlight of the whole event was the fact that I was the *sarbala*, which meant that I was to be with the bridegroom till he got married! I got a taste of importance when I was made to travel in a car with the bridegroom while the rest of the marriage party was stashed in a bus. I was even asked to get a jacket stitched for myself, and I insisted on having a bowtie, which not many tailors in Ferozepur knew how to stitch back then. My sense of importance was, however, shattered once the bride came home and I was relegated once again to my original status as one of the family's grandchildren!

Ramesh and Veena were blessed with two children — Anjali and Alok. Ramesh returned to India after spending a few years in the US and settled in Bombay where he ran his own factory. Unfortunately, Alok passed away at a very young age in 1993, leaving behind a completely shattered family.

The youngest of the siblings, Indu was a very bright student and she did her post graduation in economics from Chandigarh University. She was married to Jitender Krishan Puri in 1966, a handsome young man from Moga whose family was in the business of manufacturing edible oil and also owned petrol pumps. Indu and Jitender's wedding was my first experience of a grand family wedding. The entire extended family had gotten together for the celebrations and as there were not enough rooms in my maternal grandparents' house for all of us to stay together, we had shifted to a large haveli, called Ansal Bhawan, for the duration of the wedding functions. Indu and Jitender had two children—Vivek and Rashmi. They had settled in Kullu, in Himachal Pradesh, but Jitender's untimely demise in 1971 devastated the family. However, Indu, a woman with an iron will, took active part in the family business and kept the family together, raising the children by herself.

Mahesh Niwas, the family house of the Vinayaks, was a large two-storey house with a courtyard and a large terrace. As children, we enjoyed the large space and the numerous rooms that the house had as places we could play in whenever we visited Ferozepur because our own house in Bhopal was a small first floor house with just two bedrooms. My maternal grandmother, Sita Devi, dotted on all of us and indulged us as much as she could. She always had something special cooked for us when we were with her. Even the family's cook, Lal Dei, or Lallo Masi as we called her, was an affectionate person who went out of her way to protect us from our mothers' wrath.

I was born in Ferozepur and I have very fond memories of all the time I spent in the town. We visited Ferozepur almost every year during our summer holidays till I went to college, and we would spend at least a month with my maternal and paternal grandparents. Those were days of great fun as all the cousins, both on my paternal and maternal sides, would gather together. The boys would go together to swim in the municipal swimming pool. We would go for walks in the Company Bagh, climb up trees and play on the roof of our grandparents' houses. My father's aunt, Leelawati Kakar, owned a theatre called Simla Talkies in Ferozepur, and we would regularly go there to watch movies. The highlight of these outings was the box that was booked for us and the samosas and pastries that we were served when we went there. Once we were of school-going age, we were admitted to a school in Ferozepur for two months, so that we could utilise even our vacation time gainfully. The memories that I have of our time in Ferozepur are memories that remain fresh and vivid even to this day.

Chapter 7

BHOPAL

⌘

This next chapter in the story of the Ubeoris is the one closest to me since it revolves around my own parents — Balkrishan and Satish — my siblings, and me.

Balkrishan, the youngest of Lala Harbansraj's three sons, was a third generation lawyer. He had studied in the Government Law College at Lahore and Simla and had enjoyed a good life. But like many others of his generation who had lived through the Partition, the trauma of the event took its toll. Being hunted down by an angry mob, disguising himself as a Muslim man to reach the refugee camp safely, the days of separation from the rest of the family, the time spent in the Amritsar camp, all of these trials left a deep impact on my father, and I can only imagine how painful and troubling those days must have been because he never talked about his experiences openly. There was always a reluctance to go probing into the past and open old wounds that had, perhaps, never quite healed.

After my father was reunited with the rest of his family in the refugee camp in Amritsar and once they had moved out of the camp itself, all thanks to the Handas, my father enrolled himself in the Government Law College in Simla since he had not yet finished his education. Once he got his law degree, he declined the position of government pleader with the Punjab state government and decided, instead, to try his fortune in setting up his own legal practice. At that point in time, however, Ferozepur had very limited opportunities for those in the legal profession and he decided, therefore, to go to the Central Provinces where his brother Kewal Krishan was doing well as a forest contractor. He had stayed with him in Jabalpur back in 1944-45 and had been suitably impressed with the town's vitality. Jabalpur was one of the largest towns in Central India. It had a large cantonment and was also where the Defence Vehicle Factory was located. Additionally, it functioned as a large and extremely crucial railway junction between Mumbai, Calcutta, and Allahabad. Most importantly though, it had a High Court seat also, making it the perfect place for my father to start his legal career from.

But all his expectations and hopes were thrown to the winds when in 1949, Kewal Krishan moved to Khandwa, a tehsil town on the border between the Central Provinces and the erstwhile princely state of Khandesh. He visited Khandwa and stayed with his brother's family for a few days, but he could not spot any opportunities for establishing a flourishing future there, at least not in the way he had envisioned. Much disappointed with this turn of events, my father bid farewell to Khandwa and to the idea of practicing law there and boarded the third-class bogie of Punjab Mail, bound for Ferozepur, in November 1949, unaware that fate had a different plan in mind for him.

In the train, while he was trying to overcome his dejection and figure out a way to take control of himself and his future, my father met Mr Nema, a young lawyer like him from a place named Kaveli. Mr Nema also belonged to a family of lawyers and he too was exploring the possibility of starting a legal practice in the state of Bhopal which had its own judicial system and a High Court as well. According to him, Bhopal could be a place with good opportunities for people like them. Furthermore, he had family there and they could ease his entry into the city.

After hearing all this, Balkrishan Uberoi was not sure what he wanted to do. Should he go back home to Ferozepur and restart his search for opportunities or take the plunge and try his luck in Bhopal, a city where he knew no one at all? The ten-hour journey from Khandwa to Bhopal was a long and sleepless one for Balkrishan.

The next morning, at around 9 a.m. when the train stopped at the station in Bhopal, my father finally decided to alight and try his fortunes in the city. He got off, and when the train pulled away, he was left standing alone on the platform on a cold winter morning with a small leather suitcase, some two hundred rupees in his pocket, and a law degree. He knew absolutely no one in Bhopal, had nowhere to go, and did not even know what he was going to do.

At that time, Bhopal was a seventeen gun salute state, which had merged with the Union of India under pressure from Vallabh Bhai Patel, as Nawab Hamidullah, the last ruling nawab of Bhopal and also the chairman of the Chamber of Princely States, was still toying with the idea of joining Pakistan. But being entirely landlocked with no boundary with Pakistan for 1,000 miles meant that this idea was a foolhardy one. He was even negotiating with Jinnah for the position of president if he threw his weight behind him. The princely states of Junagarh, Hyderabad, and Kashmir were still on the fence about whether they would join India or Pakistan, and the nawab of Bhopal was trying to extract his pound of flesh in spite of the geographical impossibility of what he was proposing. Finally in 1950, however, Bhopal signed the deed of accession and became a part of the Union of India.

On that fateful morning in November 1949, after Balkrishan Uberoi came out of the railway station, he hired a tonga and went looking for a place to stay. He checked into a lodge which had a tariff of two rupees a day and then contacted the person whose reference Mr Nema had given him before they had parted ways in Bhopal. But as it turned out, the man was not of much help. My father must have also visited the local courts and tried to meet the lawyers already practising there, but nothing beneficial came out of these attempts.

Bhopal had a large timber trade business at that time, and my father found out that there were some wealthy

Punjabi timber traders operating in the city. He tried to build a relationship with them so that he could explore the possibility of setting up a professional association with them, but things didn't seem to be in his favour. In the meantime, Mr Nema also arrived in Bhopal and the two of them decided to get together to start their own legal practice. For an entire month, they ran from pillar to post trying to find work, with no apparent success. As the days passed in one rejection after the other, Mr Nema began loosing patience and one fine morning, he announced that he was returning home to Kaveli. Balkrishan Uberoi was stunned and in a state of complete shock. He did not know what to do. His meagre resources were also running out and without Mr Nema with him, it would be difficult to stay on in Bhopal. Once again, Balkrishan was left with two options—first, and the easier one of the two, to go back home and try to figure things out there, and second, to continue staying in Bhopal, work hard, and keep trying till lady luck finally smiled at him. They say that fortune favours the brave, and my father decided to continue looking for opportunities in Bhopal for some more time. If things did not work out, he could always take the easier option of going back to Ferozepur. But in the days and weeks that followed, my father, driven by thoughts of failure and how he would face his family if he went back to Ferozepur, kept trying everything he possibly could to find work, and eventually, fortune did favour him after all.

A gentleman named Lala Mulk Raj Malhotra who had a lot of properties in Bhopal took a liking to my father and not only did he encourage him to keep trying, but he also began giving him legal work to do. With this, the doors to finding more work opened up for Balkrishan. There was another Punjabi Khatri family in Bhopal, the Kapoors, who were managing agents for the Bhopal textile mills, and they too helped him a lot by giving him more and more legal work pertaining to the mills. The patriarch, Mr Kapoor was very close to Dr Shankar Dayal Sharma, who would later become the president of India. Dr Sharma began his political career as a student leader who studied law in England with the aid of a scholarship from the nawab of Bhopal. He took active part in the Quit India Movement and led the movement against the nawab of Bhopal not signing the deed of accession after India's independence. For his stand against the nawab, Dr Sharma was even sent to prison, but the tables turned when Bhopal joined the Union of India and he was appointed the first chief minister of the state of Bhopal.

By late 1950, Balkrishan Uberoi was able to establish his fledgling legal practice in Bhopal. He rented a small premise on the first floor of a building in a market called the Loha Bazar. The room had two parts and a common bathroom. He got tables, chairs, and two large benches made at the factories of his timber trader friends and thus started his office. By this time, he had already been staying in the lodge for too long, but finding accommodation for himself in the city was not easy. Bhopal was a conservative town, and the local Hindus refrained from renting their houses to outsiders, especially if they were young single men. Unable to find any proper housing, Balkrishan therefore decided to shift into his office room itself to save on having to pay rent for two places. During the day, the

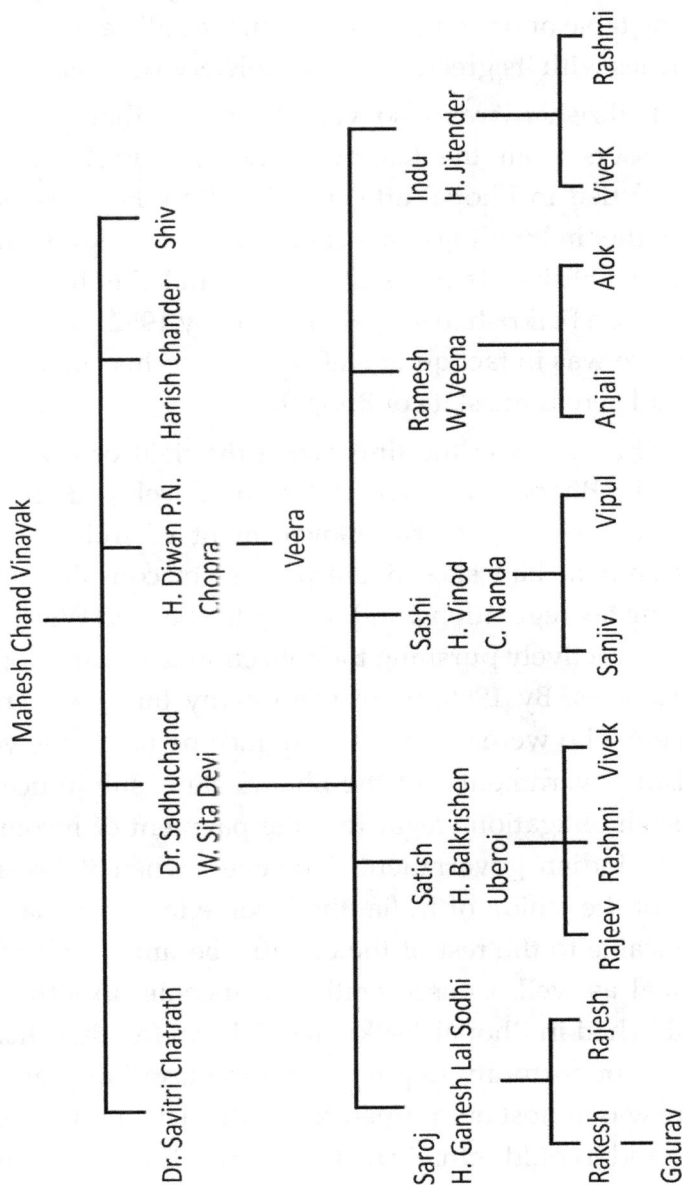

Mahesh Chand Vinayak

Dr. Savitri Chatrath

Dr. Sadhuchand
W. Sita Devi

H. Diwan P.N.
Chopra — Veera

Harish Chander

Shiv

Saroj
H. Ganesh Lal Sodhi

Satish
H. Balkrishen
Uberoi

Sashi
H. Vinod
C. Nanda

Ramesh
W. Veena

Indu
H. Jitender

Rakesh — Rajesh
Gaurav

Rajeev — Rashmi — Vivek

Sanjiv — Vipul

Anjali — Alok

Vivek — Rashmi

space functioned as his office and at night, he slept either on the table or on the bench. In fact, we still have one of the benches with its green rexine upholstery with us!

Balkrishan was also very fortunate that one of his professors from the Lahore University, Prof. Malhotra, had settled in Bhopal after the Partition. He now helped my father in building connections and networking with the well established families of Bhopal, and this had a great impact on Balkrishan's legal practice. By 1952, Balkrishan's practice was in fact quite well set up and his clientele was spread across the state of Bhopal.

This was also the time when the field of income tax laws in Bhopal was still not fully developed. In 1935, with the passing of the Government of India Act, the government had started the process of consolidating its income tax regulations, and during the Second World War, it began actively pursuing the collection of income tax from its subjects. By 1950, there were many businessmen and traders who were obliged to pay income tax to the young Indian government, but the Bhopal state, sub judice, had no such obligations regarding the payment of income tax to the Indian government. However, when it became a part of the Union of India, the income tax laws that were applicable to the rest of the country became applicable to Bhopal as well. Consequently, an income tax office was established in Bhopal. Balkrishan Uberoi felt that this was a good opportunity to pursue income taxation practice as there was almost no competition in the field at that point in time and it could actually turn out to be a huge opportunity. His hunch proved to be quite true.

Dr Sadhu Chand and Sita Devi,
Rajeev's maternal grandparents

Dr Sadhu Chand and Sita Devi, with their five children
Standing: Satish Bala and Saroj with little Indu in her arms
Sitting: Dr Sadhu Chand, Ramesh, Sita Devi and Sashi

Karta Krishan Uberoi, with Pradeep

A family picture after Rashmi's wedding, 1981

Swatantra Chopra and Baldev Raj Chopra

R.R. Chopra and Promila Chopra
with daughter, Premlata

Smt Sushila Devi (Bhabhi-ji)

Sita Devi Vinayak,
Rajeev's maternal grandmother

Service Certificate issued to Balkrishan Uberoi in 1945

Mrs Satish Uberoi, Chairperson — Inner Wheel Club

Balkrishan and Satish Bala, 1953

Balkrishan Uberoi in Bhopal, 1955

In Bhopal with friends, 1960:
Standing: Balkrishan Uberoi and Hardeep Singh
Sitting: R.R. Chopra, Gurbans Singh and Mr Verma

Vandana and Rajeev's wedding, 1983

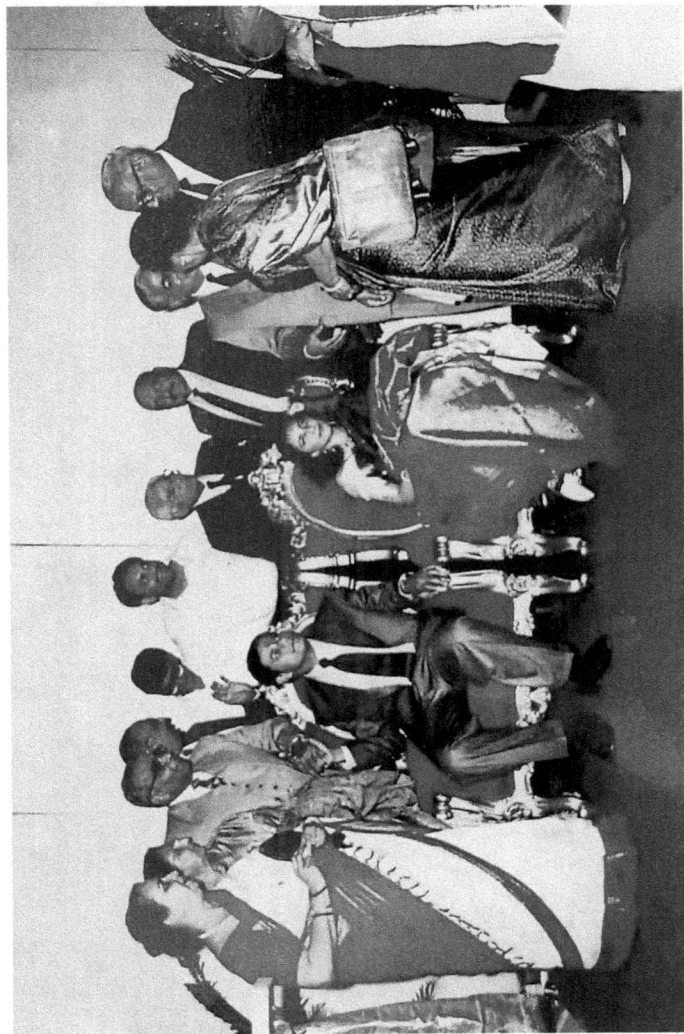

Jyoti and Vivek's wedding, 1993

Three generations of the Uberoi's, in 1988:
Kanav Rishi, Balkrishan (sitting), and Rajeev,
at our residence: E-1/62, Arera Colony, Bhopal

A family picture taken on Rajeev's father Balkrishan Uberoi's 75th birthday, in 2000

The extended Vinayak family

Rajeev's mother, Satish Bala Uberoi with Balram Jhakhar,
the then Governor of Madhya Pradesh

Satish Bala, with the Governor of Madhya Pradesh,
receiving an award for her contribution to Hindi

The Vinayak siblings celebrating the 75th birthday of Ramesh Indu Puri

L to R: Saroj Sondhi, Satish Uberoi, Vinod Nanda, Ramesh Vinayak and Veena Vinayak

The Income Tax Practitioners Study Circle

Jung Bahadur (Bahadur Bhaiya)

Balkrishan Uberoi was a very well groomed and friendly person. His personality was very pleasing and he was always ready to extend help to all. His management of his social relationships was par excellence and he made friends across all sections of the society, from Hindu traders and landlords to members of the Muslims gentry and people close to the nawab of Bhopal. He was always dressed in Western clothes and spoke very good English, and soon enough, he was appointed as the tax advisor to HH Nawab Hamidullah Khan of Bhopal. In fact, some years later, he was also appointed as the income tax advisor to the governor of Madhya Pradesh, Mr K.C. Reddy.

My father was a very frugal man even after his legal practice took off and he began earning well. This could, of course, be traced back to the fact that the family had seen very difficult times since the Partition and picking up the pieces of their lives again had been quite hard. But because of his financial caution, he was able to save enough money to help his father in getting his two younger sisters married. He was also able to take care of his own wedding expenses as well.

My parents' marriage was solemnised in Ferozepur in February 1953, and the young couple travelled to Simla for their honeymoon. That my father was an extremely social man was made strongly evident to my mother when while still on their honeymoon in Simla, he called on his uncle, Bhimsen Sachar, who was the chief minister of Punjab! The socialisation didn't stop there. He even met his friends from the law college in Simla, the parents of his elder sister-in-law Sharda, who were living in Simla at that time, and on their way back, made sure to spend some time with his wife's brother Ramesh who was then studying at Lawrence School, Sanawar.

When the couple finally arrived in Bhopal by the Punjab Mail, they found that Balkrishan Uberoi's mentor and friend, Kapoor Bhai, had sent his secretary and a car, a big DeSoto, to receive the couple at the railway station, and for the next few days they stayed with the Kapoor family in their bungalow on Shyamla Hill. What my mother probably didn't know at that point in time was that the days ahead would be much more harder to get through than she had anticipated, and that the generosity the Kapoors had extended towards them would be, in retrospect, a huge blessing for her.

Satish was a very bright student and was a good sportsperson and an orator too. She was religious, strongly nationalist in her outlook, and grounded in the moral values that her family had instilled in her. She believed that her values were the source of her strength. But when she finally moved to her husband's office-cum-residence in Loha Bazar, Satish felt her whole world change overnight. It would not be incorrect to say that the move from Ferozepur to Bhopal was a watershed event in Satish's life. Not only did this shift take Satish out of Punjab, but it also took her to a much smaller Muslim-dominated city where the culture was radically different from what she was used to. Where she was so well educated, with a BA and a BEd degree already under her belt, the Muslim women in Bhopal still observed purdah and wore burkhas. It was a big culture shock for my mother. The life she had led in Ferozepur had been a very comfortable one — her family was well respected and wealthy, and she had not lacked for anything. Now, in Bhopal, with Balkrishan just starting out on his career and still setting things up, things were different. It is quite likely that the initial years of my parents' marriage must have been very challenging and difficult. However, in time, things did settle down and the couple was able to establish themselves very well in all aspects, financially, socially, as well as on the professional front.

My parents stayed in the Loha Bazar setup for about a month or so. My father managed to acquire another room in the same building and that served as the couple's makeshift kitchen. A kerosene stove was purchased for my mother to cook on. Within a month, however, my parents found a house on the first floor of a newly constructed building owned by a *seth ji* who lived next door. They quickly moved into the new house and began setting up their family home in Bhopal in earnest. The household goods that had been given to them in their marriage were now transported from Ferozepur to Bhopal, and slowly but surely, the house began to get transformed into a home.

Even though she was busy setting up their home, Satish wanted to pursue her education, and Balkrishan encouraged her. She joined the recently established Law College in the city, where for the first time, women were now being given admission. The Law College was housed in a majestic building overlooking a lake at the outskirts of Bhopal. This building had been built in 1909 and was named Minto Hall to commemorate the visit of Lord Minto, the then viceroy of India, to Bhopal. Satish travelled to the college by a tonga, which had a curtain drawn around it to shield its occupants from the gaze of those outside, since most women in Bhopal still followed the *purdah* tradition.

By 1956, when she was in her final year of law, my parents were expecting their first child. As tradition demanded, a pregnant woman would generally go back to her parents' house for the delivery. So, my mother went to Ferozepur for her delivery and I was born in January 1956. She came back to Bhopal in April and settled back into the routine of her life with her husband and her little baby. By now, Balkrishan had started earning quite well and he had purchased a three-storey house in Jehangirabad from a gentleman named Hakim Sahib, who was migrating to Pakistan. He also purchased a few plots in the Qutbi colony which was located next to the Lower Lake of Bhopal and built a bungalow there with his friend Mr Chopra. This was not all. My father also purchased plots in the Idgah Hills area and in Obaidullahganj which was about 30 miles from Bhopal. It was probably because he and his family had lost everything during the Partition, their home, their property, their valuables, their clothes, that made him insecure and drove him to acquire as many properties as he possibly could, so that even if he was forced to give one up, he would have others to fall back on.

In October 1959, Balkrishan and Satish were blessed with a second child, a daughter. In the three years since my birth, Balkrishan had established himself as a leading tax advisor in Bhopal. What gave further fillip to his practice was the creation of the state of Madhya Pradesh on 1 November

1956 with Bhopal as the capital, and the establishment of Bharat Heavy Electrical Limited (BHEL), a public sector undertaking, at Bhopal. Both these developments boosted the economic growth of Bhopal, and that had a direct impact on Balkrishan's profession.

Within a decade of having set up his legal practice in Bhopal, Balkrishan and his young family were well settled in the city. He had acquired quite a few properties around Bhopal and was counted amongst the city's wealthy people. My father was very far-sighted and he knew that along with a professional income, he needed some additional sources of income to be truly financially stable.

In 1960, under the new masterplan that had been launched for Bhopal, an area called New Market was being developed along the lines of Connaught Place in Delhi. Plots were being auctioned in this new locality and my father, along with his friends Mr Chopra and Mr Talwar, bid for some plots and managed to acquire them. New Market was meant to be a large marketplace with residences on the first and second floors of the buildings that would be constructed there. Later, however, Mr Talwar decided to shift to Delhi and Mr Chopra built his bungalow in the Qutbi colony. Both of them sold their plots in New Market to Balkrishan who decided that it was time to build a house for his family in New Market. They had been living in rented accommodations for far too long now even though he owned many properties, plus the family had grown in size and they could definitely use a larger living space. The construction at New Market effectively started in 1962, but it was delayed on account of the Indo-China War that broke out the same year. At that time, the supply of steel and cement was controlled by the government, and special permits had to be obtained for the procurement of both. Balkrishan, being the well connected enterprising man that he was, managed to get the necessary permissions and all the steel and cement that was needed for the construction of the family's home was brought and stored safely on an open plot of land next to Mr Chopra's bungalow in Professors' Colony.

It was Satish who took over the responsibility of getting the family home constructed in New Market. As they didn't own any personal means of transport yet, she would get up really early in the morning, prepare food for the family, and then use public transport to reach the construction site. There weren't too many buses that ran on the route to New Market, which made it doubly harder for my mother to commute back and forth, and on most evenings, she would only be back by around six. These were challenging times for the family. Balkrishan was working even harder than before as more money was required to fund the construction of the New Market house, which was, in retrospect, a much more ambitious project than what he could chew. Therefore, the building of the family home was completed in phases, with bits and portions being added when the family could afford additional construction expenses.

At home, the couple's little daughter, who was just three or four years old at that time, needed attention. With Satish focussing on getting the family's house constructed and Balkrishan working longer hours than before to meet the financial burdens, it was becoming difficult for the couple to manage things at home. Balkrishan therefore decided to request his paternal aunt Balwant Chopra, a widow, to come and stay with the family for some time. Her presence in the household would ease their troubles a little.

Finally, in 1964, the family shifted to the ground floor of the New Market house even though the building was still under construction. Although my sister and I were very young, we could still feel the financial crunch our parents were in. My father sold off the plots he had acquired in Obaidullahganj and Idgah Hills to complete the construction work as quickly as possible. Parallel efforts were also made to look for suitable tenants for the commercial showroom space in the front part of the building. The first break came when Remington Rand, a multinational company, signed a lease with my father as his tenant. This was a huge relief for him because the monthly rent went a long way in helping him financially. During this period, not only was Satish pregnant with their third child, but she also fell ill. It was a difficult pregnancy and Satish's elder sister Saroj came and stayed with us for a couple of months. My brother Vivek was born in July 1966, and by then my sister and I were both going to school.

In the years after my brother's birth, things began looking up for our family. My father's practice expanded and he hired an assistant and a lawyer to deal with the growing volume of work. The state government introduced commercial taxes and this gave further encouragement to my father's work. Soon, more tenants came on board and the family shifted from the ground floor to the second floor. While things were now running smoothly on all fronts for the family, my father received a government notice stating that if construction was not commenced soon on the plot that he had purchased in 1960 and which was still lying unused, his ownership of the same would be cancelled.

The plot in question was the one that lay adjacent to the building we were living in. But starting construction on it meant a huge investment outlay. However, as there was no other way out to save the plot, Balkrishan started the construction of a building on that parcel of land towards the end of 1968. This time round, the logistical challenges of overseeing construction work were less as we were living right next door. It took almost two years for my parents to complete the construction of this building which was bigger than the one we were living in. Once again, there were financial challenges that had to be met head-on, and once again my parents followed the same modus operandi of getting tenants and completing the construction on the property in phases. At one point in time, top companies like Remington Rand, New India Assurance, Indian Oil Corporation, State Bank of India, Rallis India, Food Corporation of India, etc. were our tenants. The rents, I am told, were lower than the market rates but the companies were all top notch.

By this time, the family was larger with three young children to look after, and with both my parents so busy with work, they felt the need for a full-time help at home. And that is how a Nepalese man named Jang Bahadur came into our family and stayed with us till his death. Jang

Bahadur was a very good human being. He was extremely hard working, devoted, and trustworthy. My father often said that Bahadur played a very important role in our family's success and in keeping us all safe and healthy. My siblings and I were all literally brought up by him, and we fondly called him Bahadur Bhaiya. In fact, so vital was he to our family, that even our relatives and friends, and in the later years even the grandchildren, everyone loved and respected Bahadur Bhaiya greatly. He stayed with our family through our journey from our time in Malipura in Old Bhopal to the house in New Market and then the bungalow in Arera Colony. He had his own share of disagreements with the family over the years, but in spite of everything, he remained a part of the family till his death.

After my father's sad demise, Bahadur bhaiya told everyone that he was there to now take care of my mother as Papa ji, which is how he referred to my father, had told him to do so. It was while we were all away that he passed away. We had come to Bhopal to take my mother with us to Bombay so she could spend time with us and with her grandchildren. Bahadur Bhaiya was a little unwell at that time and he did not want my mother to go just then. But we did go back to Bombay, and two days after our departure, we got the news that Bahadur Bhaiya had passed away in his sleep. My wife Vandana and I immediately took the evening flight to Bhopal and performed Bahadur Bhaiya's last rites the way we would have done for any family member. The entire family was very saddened by his death, as were our friends and relatives. He was, after all, a part of the family. We drove to Hoshangabad once the funeral rituals were complete to immerse his ashes in the Narmada. The story of our family's history cannot be considered complete without talking about Bahadur Bhaiya, and all of us will be eternally grateful for his contribution in protecting and nurturing the family.

Returning to my parents, by the late 1960s, Balkrishan and Satish had a large circle of friends in Bhopal. From people in the world of business, and industry to those in the bureaucracy, they were friends with everyone. They were active in the Bhopal chapters of various organisations like the Lions Club, the Arya Samaj, the Arera Club, All India Women's Conference, the Red Cross Society, and the Punjabi Samaj. Balkrishan took an active part in the city's Bar Association. His friend circle was extensive and included his clients, businessmen, professionals, and bureaucrats. I remember my parents hosting numerous parties for their social circle. When the mundan ceremony of my brother Vivek was held, it was quite a big event in the city. Many family members came from across the country. The then governor of Madhya Pradesh, KCC Reddy and First Lady Sarojamma Reddy, also graced the occasion. That same year, my father bought his first car, a black Ambassador from Delhi, and managed to get a unique number as well: DLK-3456! Interestingly, after my father purchased this car, my mother learned driving and she was one of the few women who drove around in Bhopal at that time. This was, no doubt, a big leap from having to travel in a curtained tonga as she had done when she had first come to Bhopal.

Balkrishan Uberoi was a very social and helpful individual. He came to Bhopal, Bhopal without knowing anyone, but in a short period of time he built life-long friendships with many and became a leading lawyer in the city. He was very humble and believed very strongly in nurturing family relations. He was well respected respected by all the communities in Bhopal, including conservative Hindus, and was looked up to by many as a well-educated, well-groomed, and forward-looking person. There were many rich people who wanted their children to be educated well and he offered to get them admitted in good schools and colleges and often personally accompanied them, as he did, for instance, for the son of Mr Paliwal of Ashta, taking him to Dehradun where he had gained admission in a good school.

One of his good friend was Mr Israr Masood, a wealthy businessman who would send us tiffins packed with sumptuous food every Eid. Another person my father helped was Mrs Hafiz, who lost her husband but was brave enough to want to run his engineering company. Such was his persona that it earned him great respect and recognition.

While we were growing up in Bhopal, many of our family friends were people who, like us, had settled in Bhopal after Partition. Few were from Lahore, Sheikhupura, and Gujranwala. Prof. Malhotra, who taught my father economics at Government College, Lahore had settled in Bhopal. His daughter Shweta Malhotra was a renowned singer. Mr Avtar Singh who was from Gujranwala was a close friend and he ofgen gave me rides on his motorcycle. Another family from Sheikhupura was that of Sardar Bhagwan Singh, who was in the transport business. Mr Talwar, a contractor, and his family had migrated to Bhopal from Peshawar and their nephew, Mr R.R. Chopra was very close to our family. When I think about these people, I see them part of one, large extended family, who met very often, went on picnics together and had parties at each other's homes. None of them had any roots or family in Bhopal and and yet they had a very good circle of friends.

Once we moved to our new residence in New Market our friend circle also grew as did Bhopal. Our new neighbor was Mr Gandhi, who belonged to Punjab like us and had moved to Bhopal. Mr Narula was a close family friend too, and his son Amarjeet, who is now a doctor in the US, continues to be a good family friend.

Much like my father, my mother too had developed an expansive social circle. With my sister and I both in school and Bahadur Bhaiya taking care of our youngest sibling, Satish now found the time to pursue her social and religious interests. She kept herself fully engaged in a variety of activities, like hosting a programme at the Bhopal station of All India Radio, and volunteering her time and services for organisations like the All India Women's Conference and the Red Cross Society. She was also actively associated with the Vanita Samaj, an institution that was built and run by educated and influential local women for social work. One of the areas they focussed on heavily was the field of education. As there were only a limited number of schools in Bhopal, they started with a nursery school and slowly endeavoured to add a primary school and then a high school that was affiliated to the Central Board of Secondary Education (CBSE). Satish was very deeply involved in the activities of the Vanita Samaj and was even president for a couple of terms. She always felt very proud when people came up to her and told her that they were alumni of the Vanita Samaj School. Now, the school has expanded and includes a college as well.

The late 1960s was also when a massive change took place in my life. My father had a distant relative whose son was studying in the Scindia School in Gwalior. The Scindia School was a public school that had been established in 1899 by the Maharaja of Gwalior for the boys of the ruling families of the nearby states, and it was modelled on the lines of Mayo College in Ajmer, Rajasthan and Lawrence School in Sanawar, Punjab. My mother was very desirous of sending me to study in the Scindia School. Her brother Ramesh was an alumni of the Lawrence School, Sanawar, and she knew very well just how much of a difference a good educational institute could make in a person's life. In 1969, I gained admission to the Scindia School. I had also done well in the entrance examination and managed to win a scholarship which reduced the annual school fees by half. I remember my father accompanying me to Gwalior to get me admitted and settled in the school. He also had a hearing to attend at the Revenue Board which was in Gwalior, and clubbed the two together.

But that shift to a boarding school was not an easy one to make. Before joining the Scindia School, I had been studying at the Campion School in Bhopal which was run by Jesuit priests. The force behind this school was Fr. EF More, a Spaniard who had devoted his entire life to the cause of education in India. Fr. More had a deep influence on the boys who studied in the Campion School. I had always done well in school and was always amongst the top three students in my class. I was an assistant monitor and was active in sports and Boy Scouts. Going from the relatively smaller world of Campion to Scindia was a huge change for someone like me, a twelve-year-old boy from a small town, because I was suddenly in a public school with children from well-to-do families from big cities across the globe. It took some time for me to settle into the new environment and learn the ways of the school.

Meanwhile, things were progressing smoothly in the Uberoi household. Professionally, my father was doing well with both income tax and commercial tax lawyers being in high demand given the exploding pace of development in the country post the Indo-Pakistan War of 1971. As far as his commercial properties were concerned, with the centre of economic activity for large companies in Bhopal shifting from the Old City to New Market, there were more and more corporations that were looking for spaces to rent. Even while the construction of our next building was still underway, organisations like the State Bank of India and the Food Corporation of India signed rent agreements with my father. After that, the construction work had to be undertaken on war footing to meet the stipulated timelines. By the end of 1972, things had settled down on this front and substantial rental incomes started flowing in. One principle that my father followed very strictly was to never borrow any money from anyone and to make investments that were well within the limits of your own resources. This policy had definitely put a huge pressure on the family during the period the buildings were being constructed, but once the premises were rented out and the additional income started coming in, it was doubly advantageous since my parents did not have any loans they needed to pay off.

The period between 1971 to 1981 was one of consolidation in every respect. My father was well established in his career and both he and my mother were entrenched in their lives in Bhopal. My siblings and I were doing well in our respective educational pursuits. I had completed my schooling in 1973 and came back to Bhopal to pursue my graduation. My sister Rashmi completed her schooling in 1975 and went to Chadigarh University to do her graduation while my brother Vivek went to the Scindia School in 1978.

However, 1975-1977 was also the period during which a state of emergency had been imposed on India and there were widespread arrests of political dissenters all across the country. Our family too, went through a lot of strain and tension as all leading lawyers were under constant government scrutiny and things could go wrong at any time, but being straightforward people, we were able to come out of this dark period in Indian history unscathed and safe.

Around the same time in 1975, Lala Harbans Raj Uberoi, who was about eighty years old at that time, and Sushila Devi moved in with us. It had become increasingly difficult for them to continue living alone in Ferozepur. My grandmother's health had started failing and she found it difficult to run the household by herself. None of their children or immediate relatives lived in Ferozepur anymore. The only ones who did live there was my grandfather's sister Leelawati Kakar and her family and Vishwanath

Handa, my grandmother's nephew. It was therefore decided that they would move to Bhopal so that we could take care of them. Our house had an adjoining setup which included a living room and an open veranda along with a bedroom, and that was where my grandparents stayed until their death. Bahadur Bhaiya took good care of them through all the years that they were with us.

It was in January 1977 that my grandmother left for her heavenly abode. Her death was quite a shock for my siblings and I as she was the first one amongst our grandparents to pass away. Even as we struggled to come to terms with her loss, Bauji, who was an evolved soul, took it in his stride and did his best to continue with his lifestyle as before. He went for his morning and evening walks, read the Geeta, and visited the Arya Samaj regularly. He was, as mentioned earlier, very frugal in his living and habits. He wore only khadi and ate small simple meals consisting of roti, daal, and sabzi at fixed times. He led a very disciplined life and this was the reason why he led a healthy life till the ripe old age of ninety-eight.

Meanwhile, by 1976, I had finished my graduation and was pursuing my master's degree alongside doing my articleship in a chartered accounting firm. However, being ambitious, I was also preparing for other competitive exams and I got a break when I was selected as a probationary office with the Union Bank of India. I had to give up on my articleship, but I continued with my master's degree and LLB, splitting my time between morning and evening classes to acquire the degrees. In 1979, I got through the State Bank of India and was posted at Bhopal. Over the next few years, I renewed my association with Bhopal and began finding my place in the city. I prevailed on my father to become a member of the Arera Club, which was predominantly full of bureaucrats, and began frequenting the club to play tennis and billiards and to socialise with friends.

In 1980, my father purchased a plot of land in Arera Colony to build yet another house with living quarters on the ground floor as well. My grandfather had started finding it difficult to climb the two floors up to his living quarters, and my parents knew that eventually, they would face the same problem. Therefore, they decided to build a house that was more suited to the needs of elderly people. The construction work started in 1981, which was also the year when my sister Rashmi got married to Deepak Chopra. She had completed her graduation and was pursuing a master's degree in economics when she had gotten engaged to Deepak. Their marriage was the first marriage in our family and it was solemnised in New Delhi, at the Oberoi Hotel. However, the wedding reception was held in a public park in Bhopal and was very well attended as the Uberois had a large social circle.

The next year, in 1982, I got the opportunity to join the Reserve Bank of India, and grabbing that chance, I left for Chennai, where my training was to be held. That same year, I was engaged to Vandana Kapoor, and it was decided by my parents that our wedding, which was to take place the next year, should be hosted from the new house that was being constructed in Arera Colony. Until now, the pace of construction at the Arera Colony site had been rather slow, but once this decision was taken, the construction activity was speeded up and in April 1983, just before the wedding, my family shifted to the new bungalow at Arera Colony. It was a large three-storey bungalow with ten bedrooms, a large living room, and separate servants' quarters. Balkrishan Uberoi had an office within the bungalow where he could meet his clients. He had stopped going to his office in the evenings, dropping a practice that he had adopted since his first day as a lawyer, and this new office space in the Arera Colony bungalow suited him very well. There was a larger garden adjoining the house and an open veranda as well, which was my grandfather's favourite place.

Over the next few years, the whole family was busy with the arrival of the grand children. Raghav was born in February 1985, Kanav Rishi in April 1985, Kanika in May 1986, Madhav in 1988, and Karishma in 1992. The little ones kept everyone on their toes. Both my parents had more time on their hands now and were entirely devoted to their grandchildren. They were still very active in their social lives as well, attending meetings of the Rotary Club, the Inner Wheel, the Arya Samaj, the Punjabi Samaj, etc. Satish also continued her association with the Vanita Samaj, the Red Cross Society, and the All India Women's Conference. My younger brother Vivek was pursuing his chartered accountancy degree in Delhi after having done his graduation from the Sri Ram College of Commerce.

The 1990s started with my siblings and I scattering in different directions. Deepak and Rashmi decided to migrate to Canada in 1990. I got posted to Bhopal and returned home with my family, happy to be back with my parents and grandfather. Vivek took up a job with the Citi Bank and moved to Mumbai. With a good and steady job, Vivek was now ready to get settled and he married Jyoti Malhotra in 1993. That same year, however, we lost Bauji. He had not been enjoying good health for a while now even though he had continued to be independent and largely managed to take care of himself with Bahadur Bhaiya always beside him. As the years had passed, he had started to look frail, although he was still mentally very active and alert. Every day, he would religiously read the newspaper and listen to the news on the television and discuss current world affairs with us. But in the summer of 1993, he slipped and fell down in the bathroom and broke his hip. He was operated upon and a ball was inserted in the hip socket to facilitate his movement, and after he returned home, he was able to walk a little. However, soon thereafter, he suffered a stroke and within a few days, he passed away.

My grandfather had lived an eventful life. From the arrest of his father to the horrors of Partition and the untimely deaths of his sons Karta Krishan in 1964 and Kewal Krishan in 1988, he had seen it all. And yet, every single time, no matter how great the burden was, he dedicated himself to the task of re-establishing his family's stability and settling everyone. His commitment paid off as all his children and grandchildren lived good and full lives, following the values he had instilled in their hearts.

A year after his death, I moved to Chennai with my family while my father and mother continued living in

Bhopal with the major-domo Bahadur Singh taking care of running the household. Life continued quietly as all of us got busy with our respective jobs and families, until my father bid us farewell in 2008 after leading a glorious life filled with courage, valour, and many ups and downs.

My father Balkrishan Uberoi was a hospitable person. He enjoyed throwing parties and there were always guests being entertained in our home. There were so many many people who came and stayed with the family for months on end, and all of them were always welcome. Even when my parents were living in the small two-bedroom house in the Old City, it was always a full house. One of my father's friends from Sheikhupura, Avtar Singh, for instance, stayed with us in our home till he was able to establish himself. Similarly, around 1959, Balkrishan's elder brother Karta Krishan, who was working in the Punjab National Bank, was transferred to Bhopal and he and his family stayed with us for more than a year until he was transferred once again.

My father was a very affectionate and helpful man, and he was especially devoted to the family. He always said that if the family is together, then it can overcome any challenge. Most people remember him as the go-to person for anyone who was in need of help. This earned him a lot of friends and well-wishers, along with a whole lot of respect within the family and beyond. Though he was the youngest of the brothers, it was my father who discharged all the responsibilities of a family's head, from marrying his sisters to taking care of his ageing parents, he did it all. And this was not restricted to his side of the family alone.

He was equally devoted and responsible when it came to his in-laws' family.

In 1975, for instance, Satish's elder sister Saroj, who had migrated to the US, lost her husband Ganeshi Lal Sondhi to an untimely death at the age of forty-seven. My parents flew all the way to the US and stayed there with my aunt and her bereaved family for weeks. My father took it upon himself to take care of the family in the years ahead. In 1977, he got Rakesh, my aunt's son, married and settled. Later, he also got the younger son Rajesh married and settled in Chicago, happily discharging the responsibilities of the father they had lost.

There are numerous such instances where he played the role of a comfort giver to those who needed support and help, both within the family and outside of it. I've heard so many stories from so many people about how he helped them when they needed help. He helped people establish their businesses, construct their homes. He assisted others is arranging and financing their children's weddings. He had seen the ugly realities of life so closely that he could empathise with people who were troubled, and he was always willing to extend a helping hand. And most people could never forget that.

By 2000, when he was around seventy-five years of age, he starting leading a semi-retired life. He closed his Loha Bazar office but continued to work from his home office full time and would visit the income tax office a couple of times every week. He always said that a person should keep working till his end, and this he practiced in letter and spirit. In 2008, after he suffered from a stroke in the early hours of the morning and was rushed to the hospital, he was more worried about his professional commitments getting disrupted in the coming week than about anything else, and wanted someone to take care of them while he recuperated in the hospital!

My father was the one who held us all together. He ensured that the family got together at least a couple of times in a year during Diwali, Holi, and for birthdays. He visited his children and members of the extended family quite regularly, be it in Bombay where I was posted, the US where Rashmi had moved to from Canada, or Dubai where Vivek was working. When Vivek was blessed with twins, Sahil and Seeya in Dubai, he went there to bless the children.

Balkrishan Uberoi was a very noble soul and had his feet firmly planted on the ground. Wealth and success never deterred him from being frugal in his living or from using these are the basis of judging a relationship. Once, when I accompanied him to the wedding celebrations of one of his acquaintance who wasn't doing well financially, I wondered why my father was so keen to attend the celebrations. It was taking place in a not-so-well-to-do area, where we had to alight from the car and walk a good distance through small and dirty paths to where the wedding was taking place. When I asked my father, he told me that the person who had invited him had helped him in the initial days of him setting up his legal practise, and that just because this man was not so fortunate and had fallen on bad times did not mean that his help could be forgotten. Joining in in his celebrations was a form of expressing gratitude. When we reach the venue, I saw how the man's family were so happy to see us there. We were treated like royalty, and I got a clear glimpse of the kind of person my father was and of his personality.

Another one of my father's characteristic traits was that he was very calm and cool at all times. He never lost his temper and never reacted to a situation in a hurry. He always took his time to assess and think things through. An old anecdote comes to mind here. I was in the tenth standard and was back home from school for my holidays and living with us at that point in time was the son of my father's friend, Mr Jain. He was a year senior to me and was pursuing his graduation. Our next door neighbour was Mr J.S. Gandhi, and his son Devendra, or Chinoo as the family called him, had been my classmate till I shifted to Scindia school, but in spite of this move, we remained good friends. One day, late at night when all three of us were trying to study, we had the bright idea of going out for some tea. But as all the tea shops in the vicinity had closed down, we decided to sneak out in Mr Gandhi's Fiat car since Chinoo claimed that he knew how to drive. So there we were at around one in the night, pushing the car out from where it was parked so that our parents would not hear the sound of the car starting and come running to find out what the matter was. We were, needless to say, successful in our mission. We went on a joyride all the way to the railway station, where there was a tea stall that stayed open round the clock. Meanwhile, back at home, Bahadur Bhaiya had gotten wind of our escapade by now and he woke up both sets of parents and told them about what had transpired. And when we came back a little while later, we saw the five of them waiting outside the house for us. To say that we were scared to death would be an understatement. Nevertheless, Chinoo first parked the car and then the three of us slowly alighted from the car and walked over to where our parents were waiting. As expected, Mr Gandhi started off first. He gave us gave us an earful and then turned on Chinoo, berating him until he was in tears and his mother was forced to come to his rescue. Then it was my turn, and I stepped up towards my parents. I could see the anger in my mother's eyes. Her hands were twitching, probably with the urge to knock some sense into me. I waited for the same fate as Chinoo's to descend on me. But nothing happened! My father first calmly examined the car, which was not damaged in any way, and then told the three of us to go to bed. The whole matter, he said, would be dealt with in the morning. Quite naturally, I could not sleep the whole night, and instead spent the hours tossing and turning as I thought of what my fate would be the next morning.

We had a daily morning custom where the whole family would sit together in the open area adjoining the house and have tea and milk. That morning, my father was his normal self as he sipped his tea and he did not mention anything about the previous night's episode. My mother, however, brought it up soon enough, and eventually my father took over. But all he said was that I should not have done what I did because it had endangered the family's reputation and put us all in bad light. That was a big learning for me that day and since then, every time I found myself uncertain about whether to do something or not, it was the memory of this incident and my father's words that helped me in taking the right decision.

Now when I reflect back and compare my own life with that of my father's, I feel upset over the fact that I did not inculcate his ability to remain calm and collected and not overreact in any situation, no matter how difficult and challenging things might be. He always respected other people and with me, he never failed to maintain a strong and inspiring father-son relationship.

Another incident that I remember rather vividly was one that took place while I was studying in the Scindia School. Being an elite educational institution, most of its students were children from quite well-to-do families, and vacations abroad were not all that uncommon. During our winter vacation one year, a school trip was planned for Nepal. Everyone was very excited with the prospect of going to Nepal, and so was I. No one in my immediate family had gone out of India. Not just that, the trip would also entail an air journey from New Delhi to Kathmandu, and I was extremely kicked about that. The whole class was busy planning for the trip. I wanted to go as well, but I was not very sure I would get the required permission from my parents to go. Plus, there was the fact that the trip would cost around INR 800, which had to be paid in advance. At that point in time, this was a princely amount. My annual school fee was about INR 2,000 of which half was covered by the scholarship that I had won. Even before I spoke to my parents about the trip, I could understand how the whole situation was not really very favourable to my family's circumstance. While I was studying on scholarship, how could I justify so massive an expenditure that was nothing but an indulgence? But my youthful sense of self esteem prevented me from seeing things clearly, and I did not want to face the mockery of my friends. So, when I went back home during the vacation, I shared the trip leaflet with my father with a lot of hope and excitement in my heart. He looked at it and went over the details, and in his typical measured voice, said he would think it over. While it was not an out-an-out approval, I though he looked supportive enough. I was very pleased and started dreaming of the holiday. I would fly in an aeroplane and I would be the first person to do so not only in the family but also in Bhopal. Next morning, while the family was having the customary tea and milk, my father spoke to me and said that he could not give me permission to go on this trip. He gave me his reasons, but I was absolutely crestfallen. All this while, as my father spoke, I noticed that my mother was sitting rather quietly, and in a moment of acute clarity, I knew what role she had played in the whole decision-making process. And so it was that at an early age I learnt who actually called the shots in the family.

My father enjoyed good things in life. He dressed very elegantly, wore polished shoes whenever he went out, and was very fond of good food and a drink every once in a while. My mother, a staunch Arya Samaji, did not allow the cooking of non-vegetarian food in her kitchen. Though he himself came from a vegetarian family, having lived in hostels in Lahore and Simla, my father used to have non-vegetarian food quite regularly. But after they got married, he respected my mother's beliefs and never imposed on my mother to cook non-vegetarian food in the house. We were told that my mother permitted the cooking and consumption of eggs in the house only after the family physician recommended my parents feed eggs to my sister when she had fallen ill as a child. It was only after my own son was a little grown up and began enjoying eating chicken, that my father suggested to my mother that chicken be prepared in her kitchen. To our absolute surprise, after more than forty years of being against it and not allowing chicken to be cooked in the house, she conceded easily and Bahadur Bhaiya did the rest. Such was the degree and depth of her love for her grandchildren!

It was from my father that I learnt what it meant to be the eldest child in a family. I was trained from the very beginning to perform that role, and it has moulded my personality for my entire life. I have always felt responsible for everything and everyone in my family. This tendency brought with it a sense of initiative and drive and my parents never discouraged me from doing anything. So much so that when at the tender age of twelve, I had to decide which education stream I should opt for, that decision was left to my judgment. I have no way of knowing if had I gotten wise advice from someone, it would have chartered my course in life differently, whether for better or worse, but it certainly made me take responsibility for my decisions and also take charge of my future.

The number of times I experimented with my career and my education was an integral part of my progression. From doing a B.Sc. to enrolling for an MBA at Chandigarh University but not joining due to the Emergency of 1975 and then going on to pursuing a degree in law and chartered accountancy, I moved up and down through a lot of choice. Throughout it all, the one thing that my father told me again and again was to go with the flow and to hold on strongly to ambition. He taught me to never be disappointed with failures and to accept challenges. When one door closes, there are many more doors that are thrown open. One only has to look around with determination to find a new door.

My move from the Union Bank of India to the State Bank of India, and then from there to the Reserve Bank of India was a part of my upward professional mobility. Then in 1996, I found myself at a crossroad when I was given the opportunity to work at ANZ Grindlay Bank, a premier foreign bank, for a handsome salary. But leaving a career with the Reserve Bank of India, the premier banking institute in the country, was a rather difficult decision to take. We all came to Bhopal and I discussed this crucial move with my father. I told him that if I stayed where I was, I would have more than twenty years of secure service with the RBI. With a young family to take care of, that sort of financial security was something that I couldn't take lightly. Could I really give all that up and venture forth into an unknown environment? My father heard me patiently and told me not to worry about my children and family. I will take care of them, he said. If what I desired was to explore new avenues in life, then that was all I needed to do. He asked me to have confidence in myself and go ahead. These comforting words and his steadfast encouragement made me take the rather bold decision to move from a secure job in the public sector to one in the private sector, a totally alien space for me. However, with the grace of God and the blessings of my parents, I never regretted my decision or looked back.

Of my childhood, I have scattered memories. My earliest memories are about our living in the Old City. I also remember how, within four years of my coming into this world, I was given so many responsibilities to manage. Once my sister was born, the diktat was that I was to always protect her and take care of her. This was instilled in me very strongly, as was the fact that there was a code of conduct that I was always expected to follow as the eldest child. Anything which was deemed mischievous or was not in line with my parents' desires and expectations was immediately rejected on the basis of this code of conduct. You are the eldest, they would say, and you cannot do this.

As a child, and even till date if I were to be absolutely honest, I always wanted to lead and do things first. When I was four, I saw some of the elder boys in the neighbourhood going to school. I marched up to my parents and insisted that I too wanted to go to school, even though I was technically still not of school-going age. My mother liked the idea. She felt that it would keep me away from home and off her hands for a few hours everyday and that would ease her workload a little as she had to run the household, tend to the many guests who frequented our home, and also look after my baby sister. And so it was that in spite of being younger than the required age, I enrolled in St. Joseph Convent, a small school that had just opened at Idgah Hills with just three classes.

The next challenge was how to go to school which was five kilometres away and on top of the Idgah Hills. We did not own a car or any other modes of transportation, and being a small school, the school itself did not have a school bus. Horse-driven tongas were the most common mode of local transport. I distinctly remember six to eight small boys packed tight in the tonga like sardines in a tin can, being driven to school by a Muslim man every day. That was how I too, started going to school.

After a few days of going to school, however, I came back to my parents with a new demand. Everyone I went to school with had a school bag while I had none. As I was not big enough to carry a school bag myself, a different solution had to be found. My mother had a green hand bag with a strap. She managed to lengthen the strap and christened it as my new school bag, and every day she packed it with a sandwich for me to eat during the break and a few pencils and erasers. I was, simply put, thrilled.

Another incident which is etched very clearly in my memory is the first holiday we went on where we did not visit our grandparents' in Ferozepur as we did every year for two months. This was in the summer of 1962, and the family had planned to go to Kashmir. It was going to be a big entourage. My cousin from Khandwa, Anil was to accompany us along with Bahadur Bhaiya who would help with the cooking and with taking care of Rashmi who was around two years old at that time. Part of the journey was by train, and part of it by bus. We stayed at the Neelam Hotel in the Lal Chowk area in Srinagar. It was a modest hotel with a kitchen setup where Bahadur Bhaiya could cook for the family as we were to stay there for a couple of weeks. We travelled all around Kashmir in those few weeks that we were there. Very often, my father would take Anil and me to a sweet shop near the hotel to have milk and jalebi which were his favourite. For me, though, the special cream or the malai which the milk was laden with was very difficult to take, and so revolted was I by its taste and smell that I almost vomited the first time I had it. My father was, in all probability, quite disappointed with this, for he called me a *jullaya*, meaning an uncouth individual.

While we were there in Kashmir, my father came to know that one of his cousins, his aunt Saraswati Devi's son, was also visiting Kashmir. Mr Mahna, who was also an income tax lawyer practicing in New Delhi, was very well-to-do and was staying in the Palace Hotel which was right on the Dal Lake. This hotel was the erstwhile palace of Raja Hari Singh of Kashmir and had been turned into a luxury hotel run by the Oberoi group of hotels.

Determined to meet his cousin, my father hired a taxi to go over to the Palace Hotel. Aware of the difference in status, he had decided against inviting him over to our budget Neelam Hotel in the middle of the town. When we got there, my little mind was in complete awe of the luxurious hotel and its large lawns that overlooked the Dal Lake. Both Anil Bhaiya and I were strictly told to behave ourselves and I must say that we did. We sat in the lawns with Mr Mahna and had sandwiches and *pakodas*, but being rather young, the two of us were not allowed to have tea. This visit to the Palace Hotel was an overwhelming experience since it gave us a glimpse of what opulence and luxury was. I am quite sure that my father must have felt the same way, and later in life when I became a regular visitor to luxury hotels, I always found myself recollecting this first experience of luxury that I had had at the Palace Hotel.

My father never scolded any of us. This prerogative belonged to our mother, although she seldom exercised it. As children, whenever we were up to any mischief, all my father did was to softly say, 'Behave,' and that was enough to stop us right in our tracks.

Years later, Balkrishan Uberoi got a taste of his own medicine from his grandson Kanav. Even as a toddler, Kanav had observed the effect of the magic word 'behave.' One day, while there was some discussion going on between my parents, Kanav was sitting close to them and listening quietly to them talk. But some time during their exchange, he felt that his otherwise calm and quiet grandfather was being harsh on his grandmother. He immediately looked at my father and said in as stern a voice as he could manage, 'Behave!' My father, needless to say, was stunned, while the rest of us present burst into laughter.

CONCLUSION

⚬

It has been an interesting experience for me to chronicle the Uberoi family's history and record the entire length and breadth of the journey my ancestors undertook and the challenges they faced, all of which have brought us to where we are in our lives right now. There are individuals who almost single-handedly chartered the course of the family and our successes today can be attributed to the decisions they took and the things they did back in the day. There are many books that have been written on the subject of how family histories play an important role in our lives and they all make for interesting reading. Some of these books align themselves to historical forces as being the primary determiner of a particular family's trajectory. Then there are books that focus on the economic side of the story, holding such macro-level factors as the economic growth and development of a region and the processes of wealth creation as being critical, both directly and indirectly, to the growth of a family. While both historical and economic factors play a massive role in determining the future of a family, what one cannot ignore are the softer forces of change—the social, cultural, and moral aspects of life. These play an equally important role in shaping individuals and families.

Malcolm Gladwell, in his book *Outliers*, has attributed parentage, patronage, and entitlement as key facilitators for the evolution of a family. This is true and an excellent analysis. But it still does not take into account things like value systems and cultural aspects. Neither can we rule out the fact that the survival instinct of a human being along with his/her ambition are instrumental in determining the future. There is, however, a caveat here. If the environment is not right and conducive enough, then perhaps no amount of ambition can steer a family towards growth and progress. For instance, a family living in poverty in a remote part of an impoverished nation cannot have an upward trajectory of progress even if there are numerous intelligent and ambitious individuals if they do not have the opportunity to grow and tap into their potential. An impeccable value system, ethics, and family support may not be good enough in and of themselves to enable a family to move ahead and upwards.

It may be appropriate then to say that while all the above requirements are necessary to ensure the success of a family, there are also such things as luck that play an important role in putting individuals in the right place at the right time, allowing them that extra push in the direction of success and growth.

Tracing the story of the Uberoi family is a good case study of all these tangible and intangible factors coming together and contributing either directly or indirectly to the socio-economic growth and development of a family. It is an individual who is a subset of a family, and a family which constitutes a community, and then, it is the sum total of communities that builds towns and cities and finally, a country itself.

In the last century, however, due to globalisation and the increased interdependency of nations, geography and mobility have come to play an increasingly important role in the lives of people. For instance, in the case of Lala Amarnath Uberoi, it was the level of development and growth in Garjakh that influenced the course of his life, but for his progeny, the sphere of influence expanded beyond Garjakh and it was the cities of both Lahore and Sheikhupura that shaped their narratives. As time went by and the impact of global changes began to percolate down even further into smaller towns and cities, there was an obvious dilution of the impact of local factors. It is but natural that when global developments start dominating all aspects of life, smaller local issues will start to loose their relevance and importance in relative terms. For instance, for the present generation of the Uberoi family, Garjakh and Gujranwala have almost no role to play in their daily lives except for the fact that historically, their roots are set in these cities. In this age of fast-paced development and high mobility, the constant contraction and expansion of geographical spheres of influence is an accepted everyday fact. But through it all, what clearly remains consistent and steady is the influence of factors like parentage, ethnic background, value systems, ethics, cultural practises, and religious beliefs on the lives of an individual. These are carried along by individuals as they move and migrate and they continue to play an important role in the development and growth of families and communities. The journey that the Uberoi family has been on in the last hundred years is proof of this fact.

As mentioned right at the beginning of this book, my intention in compiling the family's history is to create a living book. With every generation, there are many family streams that have emerged, and while they can all trace their roots back to Lala Bidhi Chand, these familial branches are too extensive and wide to be covered in one single book. What I would like to do, however, is encourage each one of them to take a cue from this document and use it as the foundation on which they can then go on to build their own family's history. And that is the precise reason why I have come to think of this book as a living book.

A lot of effort went into building the family tree, which, I must admit here, certainly has scope for improvement, especially when it comes to the first three generations of the family. I have had to depend greatly on my own memory and on what was shared with me by my parents and grandparents, and in both cases, the absolute reliability of memory is something which cannot be taken for granted. I am happy though, that in spite of its shortcomings this book can become a good reminder for the family about their 'roots,' which is no match to the masterpiece by Alex Huxley.

Lala Bidhi Chand's life is a classic example of how a change in governance can provide an individual with an opportunity to move up in life. In Lala Bidhi Chand's case, with the control of Punjab passing over from the Khalsa Raj to the British, he got a chance to shift from being an agriculturist to being an official in the newly established revenue service. That single move changed the course of the family's trajectory entirely. Lala Bidhi Chand's movement through the various districts of Punjab gave him a lot of exposure and inspired him to constantly improve himself. His aspirations grew steadily. He took great pains to provide a good education to his children so that they could do even better than him. He also imparted to them a very strong moral and cultural education, and the values he inculcated in them were carried forward through generations to come. However, throughout it all, he never let go of his roots and after his retirement from the revenue service, he came back and settled in Garjakh.

With Lala Amarnath Uberoi's life path, what becomes evident is the fact that while opportunities for growth and progress are created due to many extraneous factors which may not be in one's control, if one seizes the opportunity at the right time and place, one can become a winner. The favourable economic environment that was created in Punjab after the arrival of the British allowed Lala Amarnath to utilise his intelligence and his ambition to the fullest, and he carried forward his father's legacy. He would probably have reached greater heights of success and glory had his political activities not led to his unfortunate incarceration. His friends and peers graduated to the next level of economic and social hierarchy, and Lala Amarnath was perfectly capable of pursuing a similar trajectory of progress. But his arrest and the subsequent confiscation of his property and his being debarred from practicing law again pushed the family back to a much lower socio-economic level. While they did manage to make their way back up again through sheer determination and hard work, Lala Amarnath's life is the perfect example of how the collision of internal and external forces of change determines the course that a person follows.

What also becomes clear through a study of Lala Amarnath's life is that there exists an entry barrier that must be crossed before a person moves on to a higher level of economic and social prosperity, and that crossing this barrier is perhaps one of the most challenging parts of a journey of upward social mobility. Once a person is able to cross the barrier, however, the movement becomes relatively easier through the next level, until one hits the next entry barrier.

Where Lala Amarnath had started his life with the advantage of his father's success providing him a firm footing, for the next generation, this was not the case. Lala Harbans Raj Uberoi had to restart the family's journey at a distinct disadvantage. But having being exposed to the higher socio-economic strata, he had a burning desire to regain all the lost ground and quickly bring the family back on track. He had the requisite education and the aptitude, and what he also had was the comparative advantage of patronage as he had close interactions with many of the illustrious leaders of the Indian National Congress, most of whom were his father's friends. Opportunity came to him in the form of an adversity in 1921, when Gujranwala district was bifurcated into two districts—Sheikhupura, which was a much smaller town but closer to Lahore, and

Gujranwala. The jurisdiction was divided and the existing cases were split between the two districts. Lala Harbans Raj Uberoi grabbed the opportunity with both hands, got out of his comfort zone, and moved to Sheikhupura. Fortune favours the brave, and that was exactly what happened with Lala Harbans Raj too He was able to bring things back to where they had been before everything had crumbled with his father's arrest. But fate had another card up its sleeve. The partition of India came not only as a massive shock to everyone, but for the Uberois, it demolished whatever wealth and property the family had accumulated in three generations. The only saving grace was that all of them survived the massacre of Partition and arrived safely in India. In the days of struggle that followed for the family, it would not be incorrect to say that the intangible assets they owned—education, ethics, family values, relationships, and the desire to succeed and survive—helped them wade through the troubled waters. It was because he was armed with these resources that Lala Harbans Raj was able to re-establish himself and the family and also put together an inheritance that could be passed on to the next generation.

If a dispassionate analysis is undertaken of all the factors that could have possibly contributed to Lala Harbansraj's success, then it would become evident that soft issues like his value system, ethics, intelligence, and hard work played a crucial role in his life. In addition to these, what gave him an edge were factors like his parentage and the kind of education he had acquired. Also, one cannot ignore the fact that the patronage he experienced could also have played a role in determining the course of his life.

When it comes to Lala Harbansraj, there is one particular thing that simply cannot be ignored, and that was his indomitable spirit. With the partition of India, everything that he had built in a quarter of a century for himself and for the family was reduced to ashes. It was fate alone which saved the lives of the entire family. But being forced to start building everything from scratch twice, that too in a span of less than twenty years, would have been devastating for any human being. My grandfather, however, faced even this calamity with determination and grit and simply got down to the process of rebuilding the family's strength and fortunes for the third time. It cannot be discounted that from every single angle, the Partition was the worst disaster to have hit the family. There was almost no parental support and barely any foundational ground on which they could build anew. They had no patronage as the family had uprooted itself from everything and everyone familiar and the sense of entitlement that had been there was reduced to a more basic need for survival. To top it all, age was also not on my grandfather's side. What one could do at the age of twenty when youth is on one's side cannot really be repeated at the ripe age of fifty. However, there were positives too that my grandfather could rely on this time round, and the biggest one of them all was the fact that now he had the next generation of the family to help him restore normalcy and order. They might have lost all their wealth and property, but the family's ethics, values, beliefs, their educational qualifications, and the desire to survive were still burning bright and strong. These were the factors which were still within his sphere of influence and control, and he did his best to utilise them.

With my father, Balkrishan Uberoi, the challenges that he had to face were very different from what his grandparents and parents had to face. He did not start his life with any advantage springing from parental support or patronage. It was only the desire to survive and succeed and the need to restore everything that he had once been entitled to which navigated his life. He started his professional journey with nothing to his name, no money, no friends to help him, and that too in a place as unfamiliar and unknown to him as Bhopal. He was not a risk taker either. He had been scarred by the horrific experience of Partition, where he had had to literary beg for food in the refugee camp, and he was acutely aware of the responsibility he shouldered of having to support the family during its time of need. For Balkrishan Uberoi, the road from starting his life in Bhopal with nothing to finally being counted as one amongst the elites of the city was a long and difficult road, but it sure makes for a fantastic and truly inspiring success story!

It may be worthwhile to enumerate the factors which made this possible. In my opinion, it was a combination of my father's intrinsic strength along with extraneous factors and fate that led him all the way up to the higher echelons of society. Unless these three things work in tandem, the results can be, at best, sub optimal.

Balkrishan Uberoi's greatest strength was that he was a good human being. He was very trustworthy and had built for himself a reputation of being the go-to person for those around him whenever they were in any kind of need. He exhibited a very high level of integrity and ethics. His value system, which he inherited from his parents, was deeply engrained in him. His diligence, hard work, and dedication to his profession and to his clients were exemplary. All of these qualities coupled with external developments like India gaining independence, the subsequent economic growth and expansion, the merger of Bhopal with the Union of India, the creation of the state of Madhya Pradesh and Bhopal becoming its capital further facilitated his journey towards greater progress and success.

The theory of doing the right thing at the right time also played a crucial role in my father's life. His deciding to practice income tax law when most law graduates pursued civil or criminal law was a big risk for a cautious person like him, but in the end it paid rich dividends. Similarly, when it came to money and wealth, he was a very frugal person and believed that he needed to save as much as possible, but he also invested wisely in property which appreciated over the years and gave him high returns. He was a far-sighted person, and his experiences in the past, especially during the Partition, led him to build a second source of income for the family, which is something not many professionals do. This decision not only brought stability and security for the family, but also a higher status in the society.

My siblings and I were fortunate enough to be able to avail the benefits of both parentage and patronage because in less than two decades, Balkrishan and Satish were able to establish themselves both financially and socially in Bhopal. It was their dedication and hard work which helped in this. They were entirely focused on providing not just a good education to their children, but also a good value system and ethics. They never mollycoddled us, nor did they let us be over protected, but they held our hands gently and gave us every opportunity possible to develop ourselves. My mother's decision to send me and my brother to Scindia School, and my sister to Chandigarh University were game changing moments in the family's history. And with the benefit of hindsight, when we join the dots, we can see that these were opportunities that allowed us to move out from the largely provincial environment of Bhopal to a much larger world with many more influences that could shape us and define our life paths. It was because of my parents that we saw a bigger world, something which we would've never seen or tasted if we would've continued living within the narrow confines of our comfort zone.

All the exposure and the opportunities that we came across kindled in us the desire to achieve more and put in more effort. We were ambitious and driven. But there were pitfalls to the situation as well, because even though we found ourselves in highly competitive environments, we had not really been trained and prepared for such experiences. It was only because of the kind of upbringing we had had and the value system that our parents had instilled in us that our desire to succeed and our ability to work hard stayed intact in spite of everything. We cannot undermine the X factor which played its own role in what the final result was.

Balkrishan and Satish laid such a strong foundation for their family that within the span of their lifetimes itself, the family made the leap from being refugees from West Pakistan who had settled in a small town like Bhopal with limited opportunities to being global citizens who literally had the world at their feet. We must note here that such drastic changes generally do not take place within so short a period of time in a family's history. By the time my father left for his heavenly abode, all three of his children were well settled and successful in life. I was in Mumbai (the only one of his children to be living in India), Rashmi was in the United States, and Vivek was working in Dubai. As for his seven grand children, all of them were educated abroad in the best of universities and they are now doing well in their respective careers.

If we go by the law of averages, then there would always be a few people who would do better than others in any family. However, in the case of Harbans Raj Uberoi and Sushila Devi's family, but for a few exceptions, their future generations have managed to overcome this law of averages and gone on to lead very rich and successful lives. There are lawyers, bankers, engineers, educationists, and financial advisors in the family now, and each one of them is doing wonderfully well.

Yes, it is true that as the global and national economies have grown and expanded, so have the number of opportunities present. But these factors do not really provide any certainty or guarantee of success. It has always been the grace of the Almighty, along with the kind of upbringing, the values and morals instilled, the hard work that is put in that come together to help in achieving sterling outcomes.

In the writing of this book, one of my biggest realisations has been the fact that most books on family history are male dominated. They talk about the success story of an individual male member or the company set up by them. The voices of women are largely silent in such books. The roles they played in shaping the family and determining the future course of action are either ignored completely or relegated to somewhere deep in the background. The little space that is devoted to women in most of these books on family history do not do justice to the magnitude and depth of their actual contributions. However, in our family, especially in the last four generations, women have played a very pivotal role in anchoring the family and in facilitating its growth.

In my assessment, this can be attributed to the social change that was brought about by the Arya Samaj movement that swept through Punjab under the leadership of Swami Dayanand Saraswati in the later part of the nineteenth century. The Arya Samaj encouraged women to pursue an education and actively participate in the process of building and nurturing families. It also encouraged men to empower the women in their families by allowing them to play an important role in social, religious, and family matters. My family believed very strongly in these tenets, and they were all staunch supporters of the Arya Samaj movement. The Uberoi women have been instrumental in building a robust family culture that has been passed down through the generations and they have played the crucial role of being an anchor that has kept the family together through difficult times. They have also been the custodians of the value system that we have inherited.

I must admit here that I do not know much about the wives of either Lala Bidhi Chand or of Lala Amarnath Uberoi. But in the case of Lala Amarnath, what one can surmise is the fact that his better half must have been a lady with a lot of courage and strength to have kept the entire family together in the long and difficult years after his arrest and then after he was debarred from practising law. Those must have been terribly testing times. And yet, the family stayed intact and eventually everyone was settled. All the girls were well educated and were married into good families. This was, in fact, a direct result of the family's association with the Arya Samaj. At that point in time, there were not many colleges that allowed admission to women. It was only around the turn of the twentieth century that colleges for women came into existence, and the credit for this goes to the Arya Samaj, which started setting up the Dayanand Anglo Vedic (DAV) colleges in Punjab.

My paternal grandmother, Sushila Devi, had done her schooling in Gujarat (Punjab). She could read and write both in Hindi and English, and was actively involved in the affairs and activities of the Arya Samaj, from participating in the *havans* the institution regularly organised to the sessions where scriptures were read and stories were narrated to children. This built a very strong family culture and instilled a great value system in her children, and it went a long way in building and reviving the family in the future. Both her daughters were well educated and both of them worked.

My maternal grandmother was a mathematician and retired as the principal of a large college. She was a graduate from Punjab University and was fluent in both English and Hindi. Her letters, written in her beautiful handwriting, have been carefully preserved by quite a few of her grandchildren, including me. These letters that she wrote to her children were like a family newsletter and they gave us updates about everyone in the family and kept all of us connected during a time when there were no emails and no cell phones to use to communicate. All of her children were graduates and post graduates and my mother went on to earn her law degree after her marriage with my father. Two of my aunts, who unfortunately lost their husbands at a young age, were able to establish themselves and keep their families together because they were empowered women who not only had the support of the family to help them out, but also because they had the strength of their education to fall back upon.

When analysing the ways in which families were built and nurtured, it is clear that in the past, women, especially in Punjab, were instrumental in running the household and raising the children. While they were mostly not educated, they played an important role in the religious education of the children and in inculcating moral values and ethics in them. In other words, they were primarily instrumental in building the softer and the more intangible aspects of their children's personalities. However, as times changed and education became more accessible for girls, the woman of the house took on more responsibilities, sometimes even taking up jobs outside the house to contribute to the economic welfare of the family. My mother Satish, for instance, was a postgraduate with a degree in law. A passionate nationalist, she loved poetry and reading. She was trained in music and in public speaking. She gave us an excellent education, both in terms of the schools and colleges we went to and the moral code she imparted to us. She did the best that any parent could ever do within their means. But most importantly, she was our anchor, our beacon of light and hope, and the one who kept the family ship chartered and on course in the right direction through everything.

www.ingramcontent.com/pod-product-compliance
Lightning Source LLC
Chambersburg PA
CBHW060411100426
42812CB00038B/3496/J